CORPORATE SOCIAL DEVELOPMENT: A PARADIGM SHIFT

CORPORATE SOCIAL DEVELOPMENT: A PARADIGM SHIFT

Vipin Mathur

CYBER TECH PUBLICATIONS
4264/3, Ansari Road, Daryaganj, New Delhi-110002 (India)
Ph.: 011-23244078. Fax: 011-23280028
E-Mail: cyberpublicationsdelhi@yahoo.com

CORPORATE SOCIAL DEVELOPMENT: A PARADIGM SHIFT

Vipin Mathur

First Edition 2009

Published by :

G.S. Rawat for **Cyber Tech Publications**
4264/3, Ansari Road, Daryaganj, New Delhi-110002 (India)
Ph.: 011-23244078. Fax: 011-23280028
E-Mail: cyberpublicationsdelhi@yahoo.com

Printed at Asian Offset Printers

Preface

There is a growing appetite among businesses for authoritative information, company examples and advice about corporate social responsibility. The federal government developed this guide to respond to the regular requests it gets for information about corporate social responsibility and the federal government's work with industry to promote sustainable development.

Publication of the guide comes at a time when multilateral organizations, governments, non-governmental organizations and other groups are devoting considerable time and energy to corporate social responsibility and related subjects. Readers should note that this guide considers corporate social responsibility to be only one aspect of a comprehensive multi-party effort to improve environmental and social conditions and prevent harm; the complementary actions of governments, non-governmental organizations, citizens and others are also necessary.

As well, firms that choose to implement a corporate social responsibility approach should note that this will involve a dynamic learning process, for which this guide is merely one source of information and assistance. Corporate social responsibility is a moving target that cannot be fully "achieved" by one-time activities and decisions. Thus, businesses should approach corporate social responsibility with a view to continual improvement, being alert to new issues and considerations. It is very possible that a firm could adopt the approaches described in this guide today and find itself facing new corporate social responsibility challenges and opportunities tomorrow.

—Author

CONTENTS

1

INTRODUCTION

Corporate social responsibility (CSR, also called corporate responsibility, corporate citizenship, and responsible business) is a concept whereby organizations consider the interests of society by taking responsibility for the impact of their activities on customers, suppliers, employees, shareholders, communities and other stakeholders, as well as the environment.

This obligation is seen to extend beyond the statutory obligation to comply with legislation and sees organizations voluntarily taking further steps to improve the quality of life for employees and their families as well as for the local community and society at large.

The practice of CSR is subject to much debate and criticism. Proponents argue that there is a strong business case for CSR, in that corporations benefit in multiple ways by operating with a perspective broader and longer than their own immediate, short-term profits.

Critics argue that CSR distracts from the fundamental economic role of businesses; others argue that it is nothing more than superficial window-dressing; still others argue that it is an attempt to pre-empt the role of governments as a watchdog over powerful multinational corporations.

Development

Business ethics is a form of the art of applied ethics that examines ethical principles and moral or ethical problems that can arise in a business environment.

In the increasingly conscience-focused marketplaces of the 21st century, the demand for more ethical business processes and actions (known as ethicism) is increasing. Simultaneously, pressure is applied on industry to improve business ethics through new public initiatives and laws (e.g. higher UK road tax for higher-emission vehicles).

Business ethics can be both a normative and a descriptive discipline. As a corporate practice and a career specialization, the field is primarily normative. In academia, descriptive approaches are also taken. The range and quantity of business ethical issues reflects the degree to which business is perceived to be at odds with non-economic social values. Historically, interest in business ethics accelerated dramatically during the 1980s and 1990s, both within major corporations and within academia. For example, today most major corporate websites lay emphasis on commitment to promoting non-economic social values under a variety of headings (e.g. ethics codes, social responsibility charters). In some cases, corporations have re-branded their core values in the light of business ethical considerations (e.g. BP's "beyond petroleum" environmental tilt).

The term CSR itself came in to common use in the early 1970s although it was seldom abbreviated. The term stakeholder, meaning those impacted by an organization's activities, was used to describe corporate owners beyond shareholders from around 1989.

Approaches

Some commentators have identified a difference between the Continental European and the Anglo-Saxon approaches to CSR. And even within Europe the discussion about CSR is very heterogenous.

An approach for CSR that is becoming more widely accepted is community-based development projects, such as the Shell Foundation's involvement in the Flower Valley, South Africa. Here they have set up an Early Learning Centre to help educate the community's children, as well as develop new skills for the adults. Marks and Spencer is also active in this community through the building of a trade network with the community - guaranteeing regular fair trade purchases. Often alternative approaches to this is the establishment of education facilities for adults, as well as HIV/AIDS education programmes. The majority of these CSR projects are established in Africa. A more common approach of CSR is through the giving of aid to local organizations and impoverished communities in developing countries. Some organizations do not like this approach as it does not help build on the skills of the local people, whereas community-based development generally leads to more sustainable development.

AUDITING AND REPORTING

To demonstrate good business citizenship, firms can report in accordance with a number of CSR reporting guidelines or standards, including:

AccountAbility's AA1000 standard, based on John Elkington's triple bottom line (3BL) reporting

- Global Reporting Initiative's Sustainability Reporting Guidelines
- Verite's Monitoring Guidelines
- Social Accountability International's SA8000 standard
- Green Globe Certification / Standard

- The ISO 14000 environmental management standard
- The United Nations Global Compact promotes companies reporting in the format of a Communication on Progress (COP). A COP report describes the company's implementation of the Compact's ten universal principles.
- The United Nations Intergovernmental Working Group of Experts on International Standards of Accounting and Reporting (ISAR) provides voluntary technical guidance on eco-efficiency indicators, corporate responsibility reporting and corporate governance disclosure.

The FTSE Group publishes the FTSE4Good Index, an evaluation of CSR performance of companies.

Some nations require CSR reporting, though agreement on meaningful measurements of social and environmental performance is difficult. Many companies now produce externally audited annual reports that cover Sustainable Development and CSR issues ("Triple Bottom Line Reports"), but the reports vary widely in format, style, and evaluation methodology (even within the same industry). Critics dismiss these reports as lip service, citing examples such as Enron's yearly "Corporate Responsibility Annual Report" and tobacco corporations' social reports.

BUSINESS BENEFITS

The scale and nature of the benefits of CSR for an organization can vary depending on the nature of the enterprise, and are difficult to quantify, though there is a large body of literature exhorting business to adopt measures beyond financial ones (e.g., Deming's Fourteen Points, balanced scorecards). Orlizty, Schmidt, and Rynes found a correlation between social/environmental performance and financial performance. However, businesses may not be looking at short-run financial returns when developing their CSR strategy.

The definition of CSR used within an organisation can vary from the strict "stakeholder impacts" definition used by many CSR advocates and will often include charitable efforts and volunteering.

CSR may be based within the human resources, business development or public relations departments of an organisation, or may be given a separate unit reporting to the CEO or in some cases directly to the board. Some companies may implement CSR-type values without a clearly defined team or programme.

The business case for CSR within a company will likely rest on one or more of these arguments:

HUMAN RESOURCES

A CSR programme can be seen as an aid to recruitment and retention, particularly within the competitive graduate student market.

Potential recruits often ask about a firm's CSR policy during an interview, and having a comprehensive policy can give an advantage. CSR can also help to improve the perception of a company among its staff, particularly when staff can become involved through payroll giving, fundraising activities or community volunteering.

Risk Management

Managing risk is a central part of many corporate strategies. Reputations that take decades to build up can be ruined in hours through incidents such as corruption scandals or environmental accidents. These events can also draw unwanted attention from regulators, courts, governments and media. Building a genuine culture of 'doing the right thing' within a corporation can offset these risks.

Brand Differentiation

In crowded marketplaces, companies strive for a unique selling proposition which can separate them from the competition in the minds of consumers. CSR can play a role in building customer loyalty based on distinctive ethical values. Several major brands, such as The Co-operative Group and The Body Shop are built on ethical values. Business service organisations can benefit too from building a reputation for integrity and best practice.

License to Operate

Corporations are keen to avoid interference in their business through taxation or regulations. By taking substantive voluntary steps, they can persuade governments and the wider public that they are taking issues such as health and safety, diversity or the environment seriously, and so avoid intervention. This also applies to firms seeking to justify eye-catching profits and high levels of boardroom pay. Those operating away from their home country can make sure they stay welcome by being good corporate citizens with respect to labour standards and impacts on the environment.

Critical Analysis

CSR is entwined in the strategic planning process of many multinational organizations. The reasons or drive behind social responsibility towards human and environmental responsibility whether driven by ulterior motives, enlightened self-interest, or interests beyond the enterprise, is subject to much debate and criticism.

Some critics argue that corporations are fundamentally entities responsible for generating a product and/or service to gain profits to satisfy shareholders. Milton Friedman and others argue that there is no place for social responsibility as a business function. These critics point to the rule of corporate law that prohibits a corporation's directors from any activity that would reduce profits.

Other critics argue that the practice cherry-picks the good activities a company is involved with and ignores the others, thus 'greenwashing' their image as a socially or environmentally responsible company. Still other critics argue that it inhibits free markets or seeks to pre-empt the role of governments in controlling the socially or environmentally damaging effects of corporations' pursuit of self-interest.

Disputed Business Motives

Some critics believe that CSR programmes are often undertaken in an effort to distract the public from the ethical questions posed by their core operations. Examples of companies that have been accused of this motivation include British American Tobacco (BAT), which produces major CSR reports, and the petroleum giant BP, which is well-known for its high-profile advertising campaigns on environmental aspects of its operations.

Self-interest

Some CSR critics argue that the only reason corporations put in place social projects is for the commercial benefit they see in raising their reputation with the public or with government. They suggest a number of reasons why self-interested corporations, solely seeking to maximise profits, are unable to advance the interests of society as a whole. They point to examples where companies have spent a lot of time promoting CSR policies and commitment to Sustainable Development on the one hand, whilst damaging revelations about business practices emerge on the other.

For example, the McDonald's Corporation has been criticized by CSR campaigners for unethical business practices and was the subject of a decision by Justice Roger Bell in the McLibel case which upheld claims regarding mistreatment of workers, misleading advertising, and unnecessary cruelty to animals. Similarly Shell has a much-publicised CSR policy and was a pioneer in triple bottom line reporting, but was involved in 2004 in a scandal over the misreporting of its oil reserves which seriously damaged its reputation and led to charges of hypocrisy. Since this has happened, the Shell Foundation has become involved in many projects across the world, including a partnership with Marks and Spencer (UK) in three flower and fruit growing communities across Africa.

These critics generally suggest that stronger government and international regulation, rather than voluntary measures, are necessary to ensure that companies behave in a socially responsible manner.

Other views from this perspective include:

- Corporations really care little for the welfare of workers or the environment, and given the opportunity will move production to sweatshops in less well-regulated countries.
- Companies do not pay the full costs of their impact. For example, the costs of cleaning pollution often fall on society in general. As a result profits of corporations are enhanced at the expense of social or ecological welfare.

HINDRANCE OF FREE TRADE

These critics are generally supporters of Milton Friedman, who argued that a corporation's principal purpose is to maximize returns to its shareholders, while obeying the laws of the countries within which it works. Friedman argued that only people can have responsibilities. Because of this, moderate critics suggest that CSR activity is most effective in achieving social or environmental outcomes when there is a direct link to profit. This approach to CSR requires that the resources applied to CSR activities must have at least as good a return as these resources could generate if applied anywhere else. This analysis drastically narrows the possible scope of CSR activities.

Critics who believe that CSR runs against capitalism would go further and say that improvements in health, longevity or infant mortality have been created by economic growth attributed to free enterprise. Investment in less developed countries contributes to the welfare of those societies, notwithstanding that these countries have fewer protections in place for workers. Failure to invest in these countries decreases the opportunity to increase social welfare.

Drivers

Corporations may be influenced to adopt CSR practices by several drivers.

Ethical Consumerism

The rise in popularity of ethical consumerism over the last two decades can be linked to the rise of CSR. As global population increases, so does the pressure on limited natural resources required to meet rising consumer demand (Grace and Cohen 2005, 147). Industrialization in many developing countries is booming as a result of technology and globalization. Consumers are becoming more aware of the environmental and social implications of their day-to-day consumer decisions and are beginning to make purchasing decisions related to their environmental and ethical concerns. However, this practice is far from consistent or universal.

Globalization and Market Forces

As corporations pursue growth through globalization, they have encountered new challenges that impose limits to their growth and potential profits. Government regulations, tariffs, environmental restrictions and varying standards of what constitutes labour exploitation are problems that can cost organizations millions of dollars. Some view ethical issues as simply a costly hindrance. Some companies use CSR methodologies as a strategic tactic to gain public support for their presence in global markets, helping them sustain a competitive advantage by using their social contributions to provide a subconscious level of advertising.(Fry, Keim, Mieners 1986, 105) Global competition places particular pressure on multinational corporations to examine not only their own labour practices, but those of their entire supply chain, from a CSR perspective.

Social Awareness and Education

The role among corporate stakeholders to work collectively to pressure corporations is changing. Shareholders and investors themselves, through socially responsible investing are exerting pressure on corporations to behave responsibly. Non-governmental organizations are also taking an increasing role, leveraging the power of the media and the Internet to increase their scrutiny and collective activism around corporate behavior. Through education and dialogue, the development of community in holding businesses responsible for their actions is growing (Roux 2007).

Ethics Training

The rise of ethics training inside corporations, some of it required by government regulation, is another driver credited with changing the behaviour and culture of corporations. The aim of such training is to help employees make ethical decisions when the answers are unclear. Tullberg believes that humans are built with the capacity to cheat and manipulate, a view taken from (Trivers 1971, 1985), hence the need for learning normative values and rules in human behaviour (Tullberg 1996). The most direct benefit is reducing the likelihood of "dirty hands" (Grace and

Cohen 2005), fines and damaged reputations for breaching laws or moral norms. Organizations also see secondary benefit in increasing employee loyalty and pride in the organization. Caterpillar and Best Buy are examples of organizations that have taken such steps (Thilmany 2007).

GOVERNMENT LAWS AND REGULATION

Another driver of CSR is the role of independent mediators, particularly the government, in ensuring that corporations are prevented from harming the broader social good, including people and the environment. CSR critics such as Robert Reich argue that governments should set the agenda for social responsibility by the way of laws and regulation that will allow a business to conduct themselves responsibly.

The issues surrounding government regulation pose several problems. Regulation in itself is unable to cover every aspect in detail of a corporation's operations. This leads to burdensome legal processes bogged down in interpretations of the law and debatable grey areas (Sacconi 2004). General Electric is an example of a corporation that has failed to clean up the Hudson River after contaminating it with organic pollutants.

The company continues to argue via the legal process on assignment of liability, while the cleanup remains stagnant. (Sullivan & Schiafo 2005). The second issue is the financial burden that regulation can place on a nation's economy. This view shared by Bulkeley, who cites as an the Australian federal government's actions to avoid compliance with the Kyoto Protocol in 1997, on the concerns of economic loss and national interest.

The Australian government took the position that signing the Kyoto Pact would have caused more significant economic losses for Australia than for any other OECD nation (Bulkeley

2001, pg 436). Critics of CSR also point out that organizations pay taxes to government to ensure that society and the environment are not adversely affected by business activities.

Crises and their Consequences

Often it takes a crisis to precipitate attention to CSR. One of the most active stands against environmental management is the CERES Principles that resulted after the Exxon Valdez incident in Alaska in 1989 (Grace and Cohen 2006). Other examples include the lead poisoning paint used by toy giant Mattel, which required a recall of millions of toys globally and caused the company to initiate new risk management and quality control processes. In another example, Magellan Metals in the West Australian town of Esperance was responsible for lead contamination killing thousands of birds in the area. The company had to cease business immediately and work with independent regulatory bodies to execute a cleanup.

PROMOTING DEVELOPMENT THROUGH CORPORATE SOCIAL RESPONSIBILITY - DOES IT WORK?

Over many decades a heated debate has existed regarding the role and impact of transnational corporations (TNCs) and foreign direct investment (FDI) in developing countries. Put simply, some emphasise the actual or potential contribution of TNCs to economic and social development via investment, employment, taxation, and the transfer of technology, knowledge and skills. Others stress the fact that TNCs have been highly implicated in promoting a style of "development" and North-South relations that have put many developing countries, people and the environment at a serious disadvantage.

The 1980s saw a major shift in this balance of opinion, as international development agencies and many developing-country governments abandoned the rhetoric of a "New

International Economic Order" and actively courted FDI. To do so, they largely accepted the policy proposals and conditionalities of international finance institutions such as the World Bank and the IMF, which encouraged developing countries to pursue export-led growth, liberalise their trade and investment regimes, and privatise state enterprises and public services.

These trends and policies continue today but have been complemented by another approach, often labelled "corporate social responsibility" (CSR) or "corporate citizenship". Over the past decade many high-profile corporations and business or industry associations have responded to civil society and consumer pressures, market opportunities, and new thinking on "good governance" and management by projecting an environmentally - and socially - responsible image.

RECENT CSR INITIATIVES

There has been an upsurge in "voluntary initiatives" associated with codes of conduct, improvements in environmental management systems, improved health and safety standards, company reporting on social and environmental policy and performance, participation in certification and labelling schemes, an increase in corporate social investment in, for example, community development projects, and philanthropy.

Large companies are also participating in so-called "multi-stakeholder initiatives" and "public-private partnerships" with NGOs and governmental or multilateral organizations. The United Nations has played an important role in promoting partnerships with TNCs through arrangements such as the Global Compact, various global health partnerships, and numerous initiatives brokered or announced at the World Summit on Sustainable Development, held in Johannesburg in 2002.

The development debate associated with FDI has now extended to CSR. The proponents of CSR generally hail voluntary initiatives as a pragmatic and innovative way of enhancing the contribution of TNCs to development. Many also regard such initiatives as an alternative to government regulation, which is often seen not only as unfriendly towards business but also as difficult to implement, particularly in developing countries. Much of the criticism of CSR has centred on two main concerns: first, many CSR initiatives amount to "greenwash", or attempts to camouflage what is essentially business-as-usual; and second, that CSR is a genuine attempt on the part of big business to improve social, environmental and human rights conditions but the CSR agenda needs to be broadened and implementation strengthened. Both these critical positions recognise the crucial role of civil society and consumer activism in forcing or encouraging business along the CSR path.

What has really been the impact of CSR and partnerships on developing countries? Unfortunately much of the "evidence" for and against CSR is based on supposition, anecdotes and a limited number of "best" or "bad" practice examples. There has been little systematic research on the developmental implications of CSR.

A MIXED SCORECARD

Preliminary findings from research currently being conducted by the United Nations Research Institute for Social Development (UNRISD) suggests that an increasing number of large national and transnational corporations are indeed engaging with the CSR "movement", not simply in a reactive sense - although many do respond to pressures of various sorts - but more proactively, given a range of benefits that derive from CSR. Many instances of "greenwash" have been identified, but CSR amounts to more than window-dressing or slick public relations. While serious concerns have emerged about the limited scope and effective implementation of CSR initiatives, it is also apparent that many CSR companies, business associations and business-interest NGOs are involved in an active learning process and are evolving gradually towards more rigorous standards and practices, and in the process, the CSR agenda is being broadened.

This mixed report card is very apparent in relation to certain public-private partnerships involving the United Nations and TNCs. The Global Compact, for example, has proved useful in raising the profile of labour, human rights and environmental issues in a global policy context where, for many years, attention focused narrowly on issues of economic liberalisation, stabilisation and structural adjustment. It has served to reinvigorate certain aspects of international "soft law", such as the ILO Core Conventions and the Universal Declaration of Human Rights, as well as the Precautionary Principle agreed at the 1992 "Earth Summit" in Rio de Janeiro. It has also stimulated discussion and dialogue on specific problems such as the responsibilities of business in conflict zones and in relation to HIV/AIDS.

As currently constituted, however, many UN-business partnership initiatives are characterised by weak screening mechanisms to select appropriate partners, and weak compliance mechanisms to ensure that companies significantly improve their social and environmental performance. There are also concerns that partnerships provide the corporate sector with undue influence in the governance structures of multilateral institutions and the public policy process.

DEVELOPMENT IMPACTS OF CSR

But apart from assessing the scale, scope and implementation of specific CSR policies and institutional arrangements, it is important to consider the wider developmental implications of CSR. There is a fairly generalised perception shared by many individuals and organizations promoting CSR, that both CSR and partnerships, in any shape or form, must be good for social development and environmental protection, and therefore, for development more generally. This assumption needs to be looked at carefully given the following characteristics and impacts of CSR:

- The CSR agenda tends to be somewhat "Northern-driven" and focuses on a fairly narrow set of issues, sectors and companies. Various social and environmental issues or business activities of concern to workers and communities in developing countries may not get much attention.
- Important gender issues often get sidelined. These relate not only to specific concerns and needs of women workers but also the participation of women in trade unions and other negotiating and political processes associated with CSR.
- Small and medium-sized firms in developing countries that form part of TNC supply chains are often expected to pay the costs of CSR. TNCs or Northern consumers may do little if anything to share these costs. Moreover, TNCs and large Northern retailers continue to impose onerous conditions on suppliers in terms of price and delivery schedules. CSR may reinforce trends involving the concentration of corporate power by squeezing small firms from supply chains and concentrating production in larger firms with greater capacity to implement CSR initiatives.
- CSR may have protectionist implications by restricting access of Southern firms to Northern markets.
- CSR and partnerships may enhance the competitive advantage of TNCs at the expense of firms in developing countries.

- The CSR agenda often ignores the bigger picture or the structural causes of underdevelopment, such as certain macro-economic policies, inequitable power structures, and injustices in North-South relations, as well as patterns of investment and economic growth that have negative social and environmental impacts.
- Many developing-country governments, constrained by international pressures associated with debt servicing and "down-sizing", are unable to develop the type of regulatory and incentive structures that would encourage CSR.
- Voluntary CSR initiatives are often dissociated from national planning processes related to development strategy or poverty reduction and their design and implementation lack inputs from key development actors or "stakeholders".

If CSR is to make a more significant contribution to development, its proponents face two major challenges.

First, there needs to be a better integration between voluntary approaches and law or government regulation, rather than the present situation where voluntary initiatives are often seen as an alternative to legal instruments.

Second, the CSR agenda needs to become more "South-centred". For this to happen, the relevant actors will have to start by addressing some difficult questions.

What are the actual or potential developmental problems and contradictions associated with the CSR agenda, as currently constituted?

Are the investment and competitive strategies of TNCs, as well as their lobbying and fiscal practices, compatible with basic development objectives? Does the CSR agenda really respond to the development needs, concerns and priorities of workers, communities and firms in developing countries?

Are these and other Southern actors effectively shaping the CSR agenda? And is CSR working for or against democratic policy-making, regulatory and planning processes in developing countries?

Unless these questions of regulation and broader participation are addressed, then CSR, as currently constituted, may do more for the conscience of corporate managers, Northern consumers and some activists than for workers and communities in developing countries.

2

Strategic Partnership with NGO's to Corporate Social Responsibility

INTRODUCTION

Corporate Social Responsibility

Corporate Social Responsibility is the voluntary role and contribution on the part of the business community towards a better social and environmental development, which is beyond their investment to organisational development.

The business organisations can be lead by large multinationals and for small, locally based businesses. While, the actions on the part of business organisations here to be ethically bound to its stakeholders, who include customers, owners/investors, government, suppliers and competitors. Corporate Social Responsibility consists of a wide-range activities and programs that involves businesses looking at how to improve their social, environmental and local economic impact, their influence on society, social cohesion and human rights, and fair trade. Key areas of concern are environmental protection and the well being of employees, the community and civil society in general, both now and in the future.

It refers to the comprehensive approach that a corporation takes to meet or exceed stakeholder expectations beyond measures of revenue, profit and legal obligation.

NON-GOVERNMENTAL ORGANISATIONS AND CORPORATE SOCIAL RESPONSIBILITY

How far the Non Governmental Organisations in the nation can join hands with the corporate in their effort to social and environmental development is the prime concern of this article. The corporate social responsibility blends the objective of social development and environmental protection thorough ethical effort.

Many non-governmental organisations in India are engaged in social development and environmental development activities. These organisations are good enough to support the industrial development by ensuring community participation the developmental process. The concept of corporate social responsibility is underpinned by the idea that corporations can no longer act as isolated economic entities operating in detachment from broader society. Corporate Social Responsibility to be looked upon as mutual support programs that ensure development of community near by the industrial area with the expansion and development of the industrial organisations.

The community today needs external agency intervention in the alleviation of many social problems like poverty, health, unemployment, community education, homelessness and eco development programs.

By looking upon the needs of the community, the organisation gets an opportunity to understand the social needs of the people and it will enable them to intervene into such social issues and finding solution to the many basic needs. It develops greater trust and confidence on the community on the business organisation effort in their real development. Integrated community investment strategies align internal community-related issues and link business goals with community needs. Here the role of Non Governmental Organisations can be better realized. The

Non Governmental Organisations existing within the industrial location and closer to the community can better act as moderators and facilitators in the realization of their social need and better environmental protection. The industrial expansion is a threat to the people living near by and it invites protest from many like consumer, investors, activist groups, government regulators and other stakeholders.

To develop a better rapport with the community in the implementation of the developmental activities the Non Governmental organisations can play better role with the industry and community. They can help the industrial management in convincing the expansion program to the community and there by develop a proactive and social environmental and industrial development policy. Lower operating costs, Enhanced brand image and reputation, Reduced regulatory oversight, Product safety and decreased liability, Improved financial performance etc are the benefit to the organisation. The benefit of Corporate Social Responsibility not only for the community and organisation but also for the employees. The Research demonstrates Corporate Social Responsibility initiatives have a positive impact on employee morale, motivation, commitment, loyalty, training, recruitment and turnover.

Benefits in these areas have been found to improve the bottom line of companies. Three surveys across Europe, the USA and a survey involving 25 countries found employees felt greater loyalty, satisfaction and motivation when their companies were socially responsible. The impact of these HR initiatives gives better brand image to the organisation in the labour market and it in turn help the HR department to get potential employees who believe in similar values system. The ultimate goal of such effort is the development of an 'organisational culture' which establishes harmonious relationship with the Community-Employee and

Organisation at large. This establishes that fact that many Corporate Social Responsibility initiatives reflect the essence of Human Resource Management activities.

Role of Human Resource Managers

If Non Governmental Organisations can play better role in the corporate social responsibility, the question here is, who can play better role in linking industry with community. The answer here is Human Resource Management Department of the industry. The HR managers should take lead in its effort to make a linkage between community and the industry. To develop better rapport with the people, HR managers have to make use of their Strategic Relationship Management Skills. They should interact with the community by establishing better linkage with the Non Governmental Organisations Working there in the locality. The HR managers can initially conduct Focus Group Discussion (FGD) with the community and community leaders with the help of Non Governmental Organisations and need evaluation and need prioritization is to be conducted.

Here HR managers can act as facilitators in the Corporate Social Responsibility initiatives. The community may have unlimited social needs. It is the responsibility of the HR managers to intervene into those needs and give a realistic perception to the community members related to their unlimited and unrealistic needs. The needs of the community to be segregated into important and important needs, to unimportant and unimportant needs. Both short-term goals and long-term goals are to be segregated. The discussion to be entertained and the need categorization and finalization should come from the community itself. The HR managers who act as the implied leaders should lead the community towards realistic goal perception that integrate the goals and objectives of Corporate Social Responsibility programme initiated by the organisation.

This indicates that as leaders of the Corporate Social Responsibility programme HR managers should integrate the needs of the community and that of the organisation. The list of social development needs and the environmental protection needs to be discussed soon after the Focus Group Discussions, with the top management in order to ascertain whether all those needs can be met with the budget allotment for the developmental programs.

A multi level discussion, with members of the NGO's, HR managers and representative of the Top Management, is to be initiated for the finalization of the social intervention programme. Corporate Social Responsibility offers the HR community opportunities to demonstrate its strategic focus. The relationship with the community and Non Governmental Organisations indicates the level of HR manager's success role in the Corporate Social Responsibility effort.

Corporate social responsibility is most frequently used to describe a company's relations with its wider community. CSR is on the boundary of HR and PR. There are dangers for companies and for the HR function if it is allowed to slide too far towards PR.

More than excessive use of relationship management techniques they should make use of strategic relationship management approaches. This strategic relationship management approaches includes the relationship development, maintenance and separation factors. After the goal attainment the HR managers should be able to separate themselves from the community and Non Governmental Organisations and lead them to new interventions and action programmes where the organisations development and Social Development can be better integrated.

If HR managers are not orienting and experimenting them with innovative areas the Human Resource Management don't have better role in the industrial sector.

HR has a role in demonstrating the benefits of workplace practices that both reflect CSR and at the same time, contribute to organizational efficiency and success.

CORPORATE SOCIAL ACCOUNTABILITY IN INDIA

The concept of Corporate Social Accountability and its adjunct concept of Social Audit are in the process of evolution and crystallisation. They underline that corporate organisations have a responsibility to maintain and promote quality of life of the community.

That the concept is highly value-oriented is evident from the fact that even eminent thinkers like Prof. Milton Friedman question the very concept arguing that it is highly detrimental to economic growth and productivity. On the other hand, there are thinkers who are advocates of "technology with a human face", and that the study of economics should be based on the assumption that ultimately it is the people who matter in the process of economic development.

The concept of Social Accountability evokes a wide variety of divergent and often conflicting emotions among the thinking sections of the population. Juxtaposed to the perspective projected by Friedman, there are others who observe that the concept is not opposed to profit and profitability, but that it endorses "profit in a socially acceptable manner". At a different level, the concept is sought to be elaborated in terms of voluntarism and self-regulation vis-a-vis state regulation. by suggesting that Corporate Social Accountability begins where law ends.

THE INDIAN CONTEXT

Though the concept is an emergent of western models and process of industrialisatlon and the consequent social problems, the Indian scene provides a different set of contextual features. In the West which has seen early industrialisatlon. the concept has acquired the force of a movement against the adverse consequences of industrialisation, and near exclusive emphasis on profit and profitability. Having seen the material benefits of industrial growth and affluence, the West has started feeling the pinch of disruptive factors that emerge from industrialisation and materialism, having a deleterious impact on the community, social harmony and quality of life.

In the Indian context, in the first place industrial growth is seen as a panacea for all problems of poverty. Economic growth is seen as the essential means to promote social development. People were willing to sacrifice their life in public agitations in order to secure location of industrial units in their neighbourhood. In the West, the public organise themselves, to resist location of atomic power plants.

in their neighbourhood! In India, people and State Governments, until yesterday, agitated for the location of atomic power plants in their respective regions. The status of economic development of a society at a given point of time lends particular context to issues of social accountability.

The Indian context is characterised by some significant developments. The Government of India appointed a committee on the problem, popularly known as the Sachar Committee. which observed: (a) the need for industry to become socially responsive, and (b) the need for legislated minimal standards.

There was yet another Committee (1973) on "processual justice" headed by Justice V. R Krishna Iyer which observed that the economically weaker sections (in the industrial disputes) are dragged to the courts of law. and litigation prolonged. where the corporate organisations meet the expenses from the corporate funds whereas the workers are left in the lurch, with no staying power.

In the year 1980, there was a significant development in that the Tata Iron and Steel Company (TISCO) invited a team of three eminent persons to undertake a "social audit" of their organisation and published the findings, in the form of a report. No other such exercise was undertaken and reported in India subsequently.

It is noteworthy that an estimated Rs.400 crores is spent per annum by corporate organisations on Corporate Philanthropy in India, encompassing educational, health, rural development and other activities which are publicised in the media.

There is also an interesting development in the form of a recommendation made at a workshop held in Delhi during October 1985 to the effect that the corporate organisations may pool, and float a national fund for promoting corporate philanthropy.

Two issues of corporate social responsibility - economic growth and social development have to be seen from an entirely different angle in the Indian situation. Having obtained political freedom, the founding fathers envisioned that economic growth (through rapid industrialisation) would facilitate the ultimate objectives of social development. Industry has been assigned this strategic role of facilitating and promoting social development in terms of a) eradication of poverty, (b) promotion of employment opportunities. (c) removal of regional imbalances. (d) promotion of industrial democracy and by these, and many other, to sustain and promote quality of life of the community.

THE SITUATION WITH REGARD TO SOCIAL ACCOUNTABILITY

The situation obtaining in India is admittedly complex, and could be seen in terms of three sets of components viz., (1) policy framework, and practices: (2) legislation and judicial dicta: (3) emerging consumerism and voluntary action. By no means the situation could be analysed exhaustively, in terms of these three sets of factors. Yet the situation is briefly described, as a background to the identification of emerging issues for consideration.

Policy and Practices: Some policy components that are relevant for the consideration are rooted in the Constitution of India, in the preambular statement and Directive Principles of State Policy. From an entirely different angle, public policy regarding location of industries (especially backward areas) with a view to removing regional imbalances and promoting developmentof backward areas, monopolistic and restrictive trade practices, consumer protection, conservation of natural resources and others have a direct bearing on this concept of social accountability.

Any review of the situation obtaining in regard to the practices of industry and business, (both public and private sector) calls for empirical data. However, in the absence of such extensive and validated data, one has to take an overview of the existing practices. Thus viewed, the "Image" of the industry in India is such that the current practices are essentially focussed upon profit and profitability without adequate concern for social responsibility and accountability. Perhaps it is the exceptional practices which get into the media thus shaping the image of the industry. But, in the ultimate analysis. it is the image that matters in influencing public attitudes and disposition, which in turn shape public policy. Thus viewed, the image of Indian Industry can be summed up in one statement that it has contributed to the attainment of great economic heights (given recognition to the variety of social and political constrains and limitations), and yet it has lost certain social sights.

Legislation andjudicial dicta: By the very definition of social accountability, it should be outside the framework of

law; accountability should be social, i.e., voluntary but not statutory. However, if voluntary accountability is missing, legislation and legislated norms are imposed by the society. Thus, a spate of legislation has been enacted encompassing areas such as minimum wage, conditions of employment, hours of work, safety at work, efficient treatment, consumer protection and safety etc.

Although judiciary is supposed to apply law but not make law, judicial dicta has gone far beyond legislated norms in regard to corporate social accountability. Thus the Supreme Court established the norm of vicarious liability on the premise that it would be a travesty of justice if the big business houses are allowed to defeat the prosecution launched and avoid facing the trial on the technical flaw.... for their alleged, deliberate and wilfull breach of the provisions of the Water (prevention and control of pollution) Act 1974. Similarly the Supreme Court observed on a number of occasions how, corporations (especially the public sector corporations. which are projected as model employers) "fight needless litigations, raising needless objections, and adopting needless postures". The Supreme Court also passed strictures on several corporations for resorting to and dragging litigation in order to harass the weaker sections in prolonged litigation.

At an entirely different level, people in high authority observed that unless continuous vigilance was maintained, "the powerful links between bureaucracy and business and industrial houses which vitiate the system cannot be broken". Even the existing legislation is being tightened on several counts (e.g. imprisonment for default in repayment of public deposit. and maintenance of proper provident fund accounts and its timely payment). The Sachar Committee emphasised legislated norms in regard to some aspects of corporate social responsibility in order to promote better compliance of desirable standards. The Committee on Processual Justice recommended that expenses on litigation between employers and employees should be met from the corporate funds (with appropriate safeguards to avoid possible misuses).

Consumerism and Voluntary Action: In the face of increasing legislation and also judicial activism expanding the scope and substance of social accountability of corporations, the Indian situation is also characterised by what may be called organised consumer movement as also voluntary action to promote what may be called socially acceptable behaviour and standards on the part of corporate organisations.

Many corporate executives argue that while they are not opposed to corporate social responsibility, they insist that it is for the state to (a) provide social services leaving the corporate sector to produce, and (b) that in the event of State insisting upon the corporations to meet social obligations, such obligations should be clearly defined by the State itself, instead of leaving it to the business and industry to define it for themselves.

EMERGING ISSUES

The issues emerging from the situation, in the Indian context may be seen as falling into many compartments. However, a few of the dominant issues have been indicated below:

There appears to be a series of gaps in the policy framework obtaining in the country. It is not perhaps settled whether the policy should be supported by legislation and state action, or otherwise left to the corporate sector. Perhaps state is better placed to formulate adequate and comprehensive public policy statement in regard to corporate social accountability and to leave it to the industry to implement the policy, outside the purview of law.

There is a great need and scope for linking and correlating, through corporate action, social development, distrtbutive justice, and economic growth.

The managerial profession in India may perhaps initiate concerted action to translate the concept of social accountability rather than to react to the demand made from the various interests, and prodded by the State. It is a professional opportunity to provide conceptual clarity, and evolve an action plan. If the profession does not take the initiative, it might lose a professional opportunity.

The profession might also develop an ethical framework (a code of ethics) which should govern its professional role and a mechanism for professional self regulation, in the mutual interest of industry and the community. The existing codes have to be activated.

The role of state and legislation is perhaps best attained by promoting voluntarism and participative process rather than through legislated norms.

Assuming that social accountability and responsibility are concepts no more vague, and no more optional, it is best left to the, profession to operationalise the concept, evolve a methodology, alongside norms for a mechanism and frequency of social audit. In the absence of such voluntary social audit, we may perhaps end up in a paradoxical situation of "Statutorily regulated social audit"

SOCIAL RESPONSIBILITIES OF COMPANIES: A NOTE ON SACHAR COMMITTEE REPORT

There has been an explosion of interest in the company's social responsibilities in recent years, and the phrase "being a responsible corporate citizen" has already become a managerial cliche of the seventies.

The very impact of the corporate sector in terms of finance and employment shows that the well-being of the corporate sector is of considerable significance to the society. In the environment of modern economic development, corporate sector no longer functions in isolation. The company must behave and function as a responsible member of the society just like any other individual. It cannot shun moral values nor can it ignore actual compulsions. The real need is for some focus of accountability on the part of the management not being limited to shareholders alone.

In modern times, the objective of business has to be the proper utilisation of resources for the benefit of others. A profit is still a necessary part of the total picture but it is not the primary purpose. This implies that the claims of various interests will have to be balanced not on the narrow ground of what is best for the shareholders alone but from the point of view of what is best' for the community at large. The company must accept its obligation to be socially responsible and to work for the larger benefit of the community.

The acceptance of this concept of social responsibility must be reflected in the information and disclosure that the company makes available for the benefit of the various constituents like shareholders, creditors, workers and the community. Openness in corporate affairs is the first principle in securing responsible behaviour.

No enlightened management can really remain aloof to the national problems such as upemployment, over population, rural development, environmental protection including conservation of resources, control of pollution and provision for clean drinking water.

Accountability of the public sector to the people through Parliament must find its parallel in the private sector in the form of social accountability which is, in the view of the committee, a mere extension of the principle of public disclosure to which a corporation must be subject. Every company, apart from being able to justify itself on the test of economic viability, will have to pass the test of a socially responsible entity.

The Committee has recommended that in order to ensure implementation of the concept of social responsibility and dissemination of adequate information in this regard, a provision should be made in the Act that every company, along with the directors' report, shall also give a social report which will indicate and quantify in as precise and clear terms as possible the various activities relating to the social responsibility aspects which have been carried out by the company in the previous year. It may be mentioned that some companies in European countries and the USA have already started to make a report of their social performance, such as, the impact of the company's production processes on the physical environment, consumer benefits, employment policy and trading arrangements, community development and work environment, advances in treatment of waste, action to conserve energy, etc.

CORPORATE SOCIAL RESPONSIBILITY : BACKGROUND & PERSPECTIVE

We live in an age in which companies equivalent in wealth to countries call the shots and control much of the earth's resources. Because corporates intervene in so many areas of social life, they must be responsible towards society and the environment. In India as in the rest of the world there is a growing realisation that capital markets and corporations are, after all, created by society and must therefore serve it, not merely profit from it. And that consumers and citizens' campaigns can make all the difference

Perspectives on corporate social responsibility / Why now?/

Types of corporate responsibility / Social action and citizens campaigns /

The corporate world adapts to changing forces / New social partnerships / The way forward.

PERSPECTIVES ON CORPORATE SOCIAL RESPONSIBILITY

In the age of globalisation, corporations and business enterprises are no longer confined to the traditional boundaries of the nation-state. One of the key characteristics of globalisation is the spread of the market and the change in the mode of production. The centralised mode of production has given way to a highly decentralised mode of production spread across the world.

In the last 20 years, multinational corporations have played a key role in defining markets and influencing the behaviour of a large number of consumers. The rules of corporate governance have changed too. And there has been a range of reactions to this change. On the one hand globalisation and liberalisation have provided a great opportunity for corporations to be globally competitive by expanding their production-base and market share. On the other hand, the same situation poses a great challenge to the sustainability and viability of such mega-businesses, particularly in the context of the emerging discontent against multinational corporations in different parts of the world. Labourers, marginalised consumers, environmental activists and social activists have protested against the unprecedented predominance of multinational corporations.

The ongoing revolution in communication technology and the effectiveness of knowledge-based economies has created a new model of business and corporate governance. A growing awareness about the need for ecological sustainability and the New Economy framework, with an unprecedented stress on communication and image merchandising, have paved the way for a new generation of business leaders concerned about the responses of the community and the sustainability of the environment. It is in this context that we need to understand the new trends in corporate social responsibility. There are three emerging perspectives that inform corporate social responsibility:

One, a business perspective that recognises the importance of 'reputation capital' for capturing and sustaining markets. Seen thus, corporate social responsibility is basically a new business strategy to reduce investment risks and maximise profits by taking all the key stake-holders into confidence. The proponents of this perspective often include corporate social responsibility in their advertising and social marketing initiatives.

The second is an eco-social perspective. The proponents of this perspective are the new generation of corporations and the new-economy entrepreneurs who created a tremendous amount of wealth in a relatively short span of time. They recognise the fact that social and environmental stability and sustainability are two important prerequisites for the sustainability of the market in the long run. They also recognise the fact that increasing poverty can lead to social and political instability. Such socio-political instability can, in turn, be detrimental to business, which operates from a variety of socio-political and cultural backgrounds.

Seen from the eco-social perspective, corporate social responsibility is both a value and a strategy to ensuring the sustainability of business. It is a value because it stresses the fact that business and markets are essentially aimed at the well-being of society. It is a strategy because it helps to reduce social tensions and facilitate markets.

For the new generation of corporate leaders, optimisation of profits is the key, rather than the maximisation of profit. Hence there is a shift from accountability to shareholders to accountability to stakeholders (including employees, consumers and affected communities). There is a growing realisation that long-term business success can only be achieved by companies that recognise that the economy is an "open subsystem of the earth's ecosystem, which is finite, non-growing and materially closed". (Herman E Daily in 'Sustainable Growth? No thank you' in *The Case of the Global Economy*, (Eds.) Jerry Mander, Edward Goldsmith; Sierra Book Club, 1996)

There is a third and growing perspective that shapes the new principles and practice of corporate social responsibility. This is a rights-based perspective on corporate responsibility. This perspective stresses that consumers, employees, affected communities and shareholders have a right to know about corporations and their business. Corporations are private initiatives, true, but increasingly they are becoming public institutions whose survival depends on the consumers who buy their products and shareholders who invest in their stocks. This perspective stresses accountability, transparency and social and environmental investment as the key aspects of corporate social responsibility.

WHY NOW?

The primary drive for ethical business and corporate social responsibility came from the USA and Europe in the '80s and '90s, from campaigns run by pressure groups such as Greenpeace and Friends of the Earth. Consumer boycotts, direct action, shareholder action, ethical shopping guides, ethical product labelling schemes, media campaigns and ethical competitors became increasingly effective in changing corporate perspectives.

The mid-'90s were the watershed years for the new consciousness in international corporate polity. This was the time when two prominent MNCs were compelled by 'ethical market forces' to re-orient their business attitudes. In 1995, Shell dumped its Brent Spar oil platform in the North Sea. Public agitation in Europe was so intense that in Germany sales fell by 70 per cent within a fortnight. Similarly, Nike, the shoe and apparel giant, ran aground thanks to a campaign against child labour and worker exploitation in many of the 700 factories across 40 countries where Nike worked with subcontractors.

That prompted the company to set up a full-scale team under a Vice President, Corporate Responsibility in 1997.

In the early-'90s, Greenpeace commissioned a unit in eastern Germany to manufacture a CFC-free refrigerator. Within six months, mainstream manufacturers in Germany were manufacturing identical fridges.

It was in the post-war period that the character and nature of business began to change in the western world, with proprietary firms taking on corporate structures. By 1998, there were 45 registered MNCs and the income of the top 10 MNCs was higher than the GDP of over 50 countries.

In the changing political paradigm, the market has begun to play a crucial role in shaping the priorities and inclinations of the State and society. There was a subtle shift from a State-centred polity to a market-centred polity. In such a polity, fluctuations in the market influence State policies, and it is markets that increasingly define a State's boundaries of financial and social activity, particularly through the World Trade Organisation and powerful individual cartels and stock exchanges. A State's national economy is increasingly dependent on the financial capital market and the consumer market.

But we are now on the threshold of the second phase of the globalised economy. Other value additions have intervened in the world market. An opinion poll conducted on behalf of CSR Europe concluded that:

1. Over half of those surveyed felt that businesses do not pay enough attention to their social responsibilities.

2. Over one-quarter said that they had engaged in activities in the previous six months that either introduced ethics into actual consumer purchase decisions or else made such views known by other means.

A recent survey showed that 86 per cent of about 4,000 people aged 15 or older in Europe, expressed a preference for purchasing a product from a company 'engaged in activities to improve society' (Fleishman Hillard, 'Consumers Demand Companies with a Conscience', London). In the UK, the Co-operative Bank report on ethical consumerism recently found that consumers expect more, as citizens, from business corporations.

In the US, the San Francisco-based Business for Social Responsibility has been working since 1992 to help companies sustain their commercial success 'in ways that demonstrate respect for ethical values, people, communities and the environment' and it already has 1,400 member companies, including American Express, AT&T, Dupont, Ford, General Motors, Johnson and Johnson and Levi Strauss. "Even Wall Street has responded to this trend, with the Dow Jones launching a Sustainability Group Index (in October 1999). The SGI rates companies for their success in managing economic, environmental and social factors." (Rajni Bakshi 'Corporate Angels', *The Hindu*)

The earlier mantra of 'maximising the medium-term earnings per share' has come under pressure from a wide range of stakeholders-employees, customers and general public affected in any way by the company's functioning. For instance, in 1999 the share price of Monsanto, the American bio-technology MNC, nose-dived due to public protests about its genetically modified products.

Since the corporate sector now controls so much of the earth's resources and because it intervenes in so many areas of social life, corporate entities must balance their right to grow with their responsibilities to society and to the environment. Because the financial capital market and business corporations are created by society and must, therefore, serve it , not merely profit from it.

CORPORATE RESPONSIBILITY: THE TYPOLOGY

Though the concept of corporate social responsibility has only recently been formulated, there is a long history in both the East and West of a commitment to social philanthropy, in the belief that the creation of wealth is primarily geared for social good. This aspect of ethical business in modern times can be traced back to 19th-century philanthropists like Robert Owen and the various Quaker-owned businesses. The Quakers "ran successful businesses, made money because they offered honest products and treated their people honestly, gave honest value for money, put back more than they took and told no lies." (Anita Roddick, *KLM Herald* magazine, August 1999)

Traditional corporate philosophy is only one of the three broad areas in which business companies can, and should, discharge their social responsibility. These three areas are:

1. Traditional corporate philanthropy
2. Corporate social responsibility, with a focus on sustainable development and attending to stakeholder priorities
3. Ethical business

Traditional corporate philanthropy dates back to the **19th** century and emerged out of a variety of factors, such as:

1. Concern for the welfare of the immediate members of the corporate body: the staff and employees, and their families.

2. Innovative contributions by visionary business leaders in quest of personal satisfaction, who built up philanthropic institutions out of their individual shares,
3. The desire to establish a strategic relationship with the State or society led some corporate bodies to invest in the establishment of institutions that fulfil the specific requirements of the community,
4. The establishment of trusts and foundations for tax benefits, which also support socially beneficial activities.

Corporate social responsibility is qualitatively different from the traditional concept of corporate philanthropy. It acknowledges the debt that the corporation owes to the community within which it operates, as a stakeholder in corporate activity. It also defines the business corporation's partnership with social action groups in providing financial and other resources to support development plans, specially among disadvantaged communities.

The emerging perspective on corporate social responsibility focuses on responsibility towards stakeholders (shareholders, employees, management, consumers and community) rather than on maximisation of profit for shareholders. There is also more stress on long-term sustainability of business and environment and the distribution of well-being. There is an increasing recognition of the triple-bottomline: People, Planet and Profit. The triple-bottomline stresses the following:

1. The stakeholders in a business are not just the company's shareholders
2. Sustainable development and economic sustainability
3. Corporate profits to be analysed in conjunction with social prosperity.

In the traditional paradigm, most corporate bodies viewed CSR as the extension of a financial input for a humanitarian cause. However, the contemporary context is more complex: "A company that undertakes activities aimed at communities (be they philanthropic, social investment or commercial initiatives) but does not comply with business basics cannot be termed socially responsible." (Harish Srivastava and Shankar Venkateswaran, *The Business of Social Responsibility*, Books for Change, Bangalore; 2000)

Ethical business is the more fundamental, emerging trend on the international scene. It focuses on specifics:

- how a business is conceptualised,
- how a business is operated,
- the notion of fair profit.

In an ethical business the essential thrust is on social values and business is conducted in consonance with broader social values and the stakeholders' long-term interests.

The new issue at hand is "how to reconnect the corporation to the social and community concerns it was originally intended to serve" (Jonathan Rowe, *Reinventing the Corporation*). Analyst Alan Reder shows, through documentation, that "marrying profits and humane, respectful management practices is no mere ideal" (*In Pursuit of Principle and Profit: Business Success Through Social Responsibility*).

In 1991, the company Patagonia Garments sought replacement materials, dropped 30 per cent of its clothing line and planned for a restricted growth of its operations, because an environmental audit of its products found that all its garments, including cotton clothing, cause pollution. Yvon Chouinard, the company's founder and president, defended the principle of restricted growth, saying, "We also committed ourselves to a lifespan of a hundred years. A company that intends to be around that long will live within its resources, care for its people, and do everything it can to satisfy its community of customers." Body Shop, the environmentally alert cosmetics company, and Ben and Jerry's Homemade Ice-cream are two other world-famous examples of ethical business.

SOCIAL ACTION AND CITIZENS' CAMPAIGNS

The relevance of social action and campaign interventions stems from the very growth of global corporations and major paradigm shifts in the polity. In a liberal democratic policy , citizens are supposed to define the boundaries of the State and the State in turn defined the boundaries of the market. A reverse pattern has now evolved: the market is increasingly defining the boundaries of the State's operations. From being a mediator of multiple societal interests, the State has been minimised into an arbitrator of risk and interest, primarily driven by market forces.

It has been pointed out that "the triumph of economic globalisation has inspired a wave of techno-savvy investigative activists who are as globally minded as the corporations they track. This powerful form of activism reaches well beyond traditional trade unions." (Naomi Klein, the author of *No Logo*, 2000) In the last 20 years, social action interventions, boycotts and citizen campaigns have, however, brought a new player to the global market. Rob Harrison, co-editor of *Ethical Consumer*, UK, heard arms-trade manufacturers admit that "the four women who did 'criminal damage' to British Aerospace Hawk jets destined to help Indonesia's suppression of East Timor, achieved more in 10 minutes than 10 years of more conventional campaigning."

In the mid-'90s, carefully planned citizens' campaigns brought RJR Nabisco to its knees at its annual general meeting, almost forcing the MNC to split its food and tobacco divisions. In the USA, and elsewhere, time seems to be running out for those who are content to maximise profits with minimal regard for the social, economic and environmental impact of their business.

New forms of activism that are acting as a countervailing force to corporate brand domination and the diminution of public and private space are constantly emerging. One such is 'culture-jamming'. Culture-jamming baldly rejects the idea that marketing — because it buys its way into our public spaces — must be passively accepted as a one-way information flow. So, adbusting (using the mainstream media itself to strike at dominant marketing messages and send out alternative messages) is the perfect tool. "In one simple deft move you slap the giant on its back. We use the momentum of the enemy," says Kalle Lasn, editor, Adbusters magazine, Vancouver. For a growing number of young activists in the USA and Europe, *adbusting* is the appropriate tool with which to register disapproval of the multinational corporations that have "so aggressively stalked them as shoppers, and so unceremoniously dumped them as workers".

The Internet has rapidly become the tool of choice for spreading information about multinationals around the world. For example, each day information about Nike flows freely via e-mail between the US National Labour Committee and Campaign for Labour Rights; the Dutch-based Clean Clothes Campaign; the Australian Fairwear Campaign and many others spread throughout the world.

In a September 1997 press release, Nike dismissed its critics as 'fringe groups'. But by March 1998 it was ready to treat Nike's online critics with more respect. It introduced yet another package of labour reforms and admitted, "You make changes because it's the right thing to do. But obviously our actions have been accelerated because of the World Wide Web." ('Sites for Sore Consumers', *Washington Post,*

March 29, 1998) The thing every company fears most "is becoming the target of a powerful single-issue campaign group. So, rather than wait for it to happen, managers are taking pre-emptive action in the form of environmental product development and labelling, or engaging in such ideas as codes of conduct and social audits." (Rob Harrison, 'Consumers can make all the difference', 2000)

When this public resistance began taking shape in the western world in the mid-'90s, it seemed to be an activity precipitated by a group of protectionists. But, as connections have formed across national lines, a different agenda has taken hold, one that makes use of the communication networking and global reach- out. As a result of the successful campaigns and the ever-increasing solidarity between the media and international advocacy and campaign groups throughout the world, changes have been felt in corporate attitude, allowing social responsibility to be directed towards non-traditional stakeholders.

These new attitudes have been induced jointly by campaigns, which publicised the need for supportive social action, and the media, which inspired these positions and generated consumer awareness. Thus campaigning, the media and consumers formed a partnership that led to the introduction of environmental protection as part of the factors that determine company success. More recently, other corporate elements of social responsibility, such as labour practices — and, more specifically, child labour — underwent similar processes.

THE CORPORATE WORLD ADAPTS TO CHANGING FORCES

The major MNCs have, in part, reacted positively to the new attitudes which have redefined the paradigms of social values and have thus redefined the norms of business. They had to take cognisance of the new forces in the consumer market, where the consumer-citizen is metamorphosing (albeit gradually in countries like India) into a citizen-consumer.

The major corporations have also realised that Cause Marketing, development partnerships and environmental concerns make good business sense — particularly in terms of recycling materials, employee satisfaction and morale, building up reputational capital and as a distinctive brand marketing tool. The emergence and ascent of the e-economy post-1995, with an information-based technology with very little impact on the environment and projecting a white-collar workforce and neo-entrepreneurship, brought forth a new corporate leadership with a vision of its own, originating in many instances in morally-influenced middle class backgrounds.

Under pressure from multiple social forces, the State has formulated new consumer rights and environment conservation legislations. In India, for instance, we have the Consumer Protection Act, 1986.

Another significant influence was the worldwide recognition of the Japanese business norm, which emphasises the quality circle concept in place of the traditional assemblyline concept. Employee welfare is now seen to be linked to productivity and employee identity has assumed a stakeholder role. "The companies that excel today are those that restructure themselves as adaptive, resilient, creative and sustainable — as living companies with the capacity to learn and change." (W K Shireman, keynote address at the Asian Productivity Organisation's conference in Tokyo, April 2000)

These companies are increasing their profits by continuous innovation. They turn waste into new products, leasing and remanufacturing billions of dollars of equipment that used to be thrown away, driving pollution and waste towards zero, and systematically eliminating products and even whole industries while continuing to provide the services that are actually wanted, said Shireman.

The successful corporations of the 21st century are therefore focusing on continuous improvement. One example is Hewlett Packard, which leads the world in the provision of office equipment while retaining the in-the-garage creative entrepreneurship of its founders.

NEW SOCIAL PARTNERSHIPS

The leading companies have discovered that working together with non-profit and government organisations to solve social problems can give them new insights and approaches to creating business opportunities as well. Solving community needs creates opportunities "to develop ideas and demonstrate business technologies, to find and serve new markets, and to solve longstanding business problems." (Rosabeth Moss Kanter notes in 'From Spare Change to Real Change: The Social Sector as a Beta Site for Business Innovation', *Harvard Business Review*)

"A recent study survey provides the evidence indicating when and how corporate social responsibility created benefits for corporations. The study also mentions some examples of benefits cited in the areas of marketing, shareholder value, human resources and innovation." (John Weiser-S ZadekIn ,'Conversations with Disbelievers', USA)

1. London-based Diageo plc reported that between 1994 and 1998, 22 cause-related marketing projects helped it raise $600,000 for causes while increasing sales of tracked brands by 17 per cent.
2. A recent study by Interbrand concluded that a full one-quarter of the world's total financial wealth is tied up in intangible assets such as reputation, brand

equity, strategic positioning, alliances, knowledge and the like.

3. Monsanto's experience in introducing genetically modified seeds dramatically illustrates the tremendous negative impact on stockholder value, brand equity, and reputation that can be caused when a company is perceived to be behaving in ways that are socially irresponsible.
4. The National Leadership Council (Washington DC) analysed company-sponsored school-to-work programmes and found a positive return on investment in most of the companies studied. Programmes resulted in reduced recruitment costs, reduced training and supervision costs, reduced turnover, and higher productivity and promotion rates of school-to-work programme graduates.

Nike provides a compelling case in point, "Nike suffered significant damage to its brand and its sales when it was exposed as having poor labour standards in its supply chain. Similarly, it has benefited by embracing the cause of improving labour standards in the supply chain, and by publicising its efforts to certify compliance with labour standards throughout its supply chain."

The UN Global Compact, created by UN Secretary General Kofi Annan, also encourages partnerships between the business community and the United Nations that seek to incorporate, in organisational performance and markets, the Compact's nine principles covering human rights, labour standards and the environment (www.globalcompact.org).

As we begin the 21st century, it has been pointed out that "the integration of social issues and business practices was not a passing fad of the 1990s, but rather the beginning of a fundamental shift in how the world's leading companies will use cause associations to position their organisations and brands for the future. Today's pioneers are turning a concern for causes into long-term brand equity." (John Weiser-S ZadekIn ,'Conversations with Disbelievers' , USA) Comprehensive social commitments at US companies such as The Home Depot, Tesco, Avon, Target and Timberland, "have become an integral part of conducting business and a core component of corporate reputation, brand personality and organisational identity. This is good news for corporatíons and non-profit organisations alike." In 1993, the first Cone/ Roper study captured America's enthusiasm for the evolving trend of cause marketing. By the late-'90s, cause marketing had become a standard and widely-accepted business practice.

According to the International Events Group, investment in cause programmes by US companies jumped more than 400 per cent from $125 million in 1990 to $545 million in 1998. Today, many of the world's largest companies are running comprehensive campaigns supported by substantial advertising and communications resources.

Today's pioneers realise that it is no longer about being just loosely associated with a cause or partnering with a non-profit organisation — it is now about integrating the concern and commitment for a cause into a core component of an organisation's business strategy.

Cone Inc believes that there are several factors driving the dramatic surge of Cause Branding today:

- Competition: marketers today need innovative and compelling ways to build brand character,
- Women's and teens' buying power: More than other consumer groups, women and teens want to build relationships with the companies they shop at and the brands they buy,
- Consumers demand responsibility: For example, in the USA, students continue to boycott university apparel made at sweatshops,

- Internet: Companies are now more visible and more transparent,
- Protection: Companies like McDonalds have built a goodwill bank over the years through community involvement, which protects them during rocky times.

THE WAY FORWARD

There is a need to develop a more coherent and ethically-driven discourse on corporate social responsibility. CSR is still sometimes seen as "green wash" to clean the sins of pollution, or "white wash" to provide a facelift to the company's public image. It is often seen as old wine in a new bottle — just another trendy name for good old philanthropic initiatives by companies. There is need to move beyond such transitory illusions about corporate social responsibility.

Corporate social responsibility offers a two-way street to companies, on the one hand stimulating innovative business and technological initiatives which would open up new avenues for company operations and focus on the prospect of touching new market zones.

On the other hand, it would give a cleaner societal reputation and socially responsible identity to

companies, involving the companies and their employees in the long-term process of positive social transition.

A multiple discourse on the nature of corporate social responsibility and its diverse practices and possibilities is urgently needed in the country.

- We can no longer be blinkered about the earth's resources, or ignore the fact that the economy is constructed on the foundation of natural resources.
- Green-washing should go beyond tokenism to an imperative priority in industrial and technological futures.

- The human rights perspective should be integrated in the very core of corporate social responsibility. The emerging role of civil society in governance cannot be wished away. Corporations are meant to derive profits out of services they provide to consumer-citizens and they must see themselves as private institutions for public good.
- All public institutions need to be accountable to the people at large, specially in the context of health hazards, radiation, genetically modified food, the chemicalisation of the food processing industry and of agriculture.

3

CORPORATE SOCIAL RESPONSIBILITY

Krishak Bharati Coopertive Limited (KRIBHCO) is the world's premier fertilizer producing cooperative having outstanding track record to its credit in all spheres of its activities. KRIBHCO has fully imbibed the cooperative philosophy and has made sustained efforts towards promoting the cause of modern agriculture and agriculture cooperatives in the country.

Having its genesis in farmers' cooperatives, social development and humane facets have always been of prime focus in its growth and philosophy – an organisation which owes its existence to the farmers, by the farmers and for the farmers of this great country.

SERVICES TO COOPERATIVES AND FARMERS

The Society since inception has made vigorous efforts towards the development of farm technologies and other welfare schemes for upliftment of the farming community. Over 1600 programmes on crop seminars, farmers meetings, block demonstration, field days, Kisan Melas, farmers visit, agriculture campaigns health checkup campaigns, veterinary health check up camps and income generation programmes etc. have been conducted which have benefitted about 2.5 lac farmers across the country.

- Around 400 programmes on cooperative conference, workshops and state consultative committee meetings have been organized with a view to strengthen the cooperative system.
- A variety of facilities like farm implements, furniture, technical assistance towards improvement in godown facilities etc. are being provided to the economically weaker societies.
- Around 50,000 soil and water samples have been tested and recommendations made available to the farmers to improve and enhance their produce.
- Krishak Parivar Sangams have been organized in 14 states on the theme dry land farming and farm technology.
- KRIBHCO has established Krishi Paramarsh Kendra at its corporate office for facilitating farmers in providing information and advise on micro nutrients soil testing, soil improvement, latest farm technology through internet and also KRIBHCO Kisan Helpline.

SEED MULTIPLICATION PROGRAMME

With a view to provide quality certified seeds of main crops to the farmers, KRIBHCO has established most modern seed processing plants situated in 9 states. From a modest production of 2,982 Qtls of quality seeds in 1991-92, KRIBHCO today provides 1.54 lakh Qtls of the quality seeds to the farmers annually.

GRAMIN VIKAS TRUST (GVT)

- KRIBHCO established Gramin Vikas Trust which is managing Rural Development Rainfed Farming Projects which are jointly funded by DFID and KRIBHCO. The primary objective of GVT is to enhance livelihood and elevate poverty of the tribal and rural population in the rainfed regions of the country through facilitating farming systems, development and research, institution building and beneficiary participation.

- The GVT projects have successfully developed JANKAR system whereby village volunteers are trained and equipped to take forward the project intervention and dissemination of project approaches and technologies so that they can act as animator for the development programmes.

BIO-FERTILISERS

- Continuous promotional and educative programmes are being conducted to increasingly make farmers aware of benefits derived through use of bio-fertilisers.
- KRIBHCO has established Bio-fertiliser Plants in order to provide eco-friendly and cost effective fertilizers. The tremendous efforts putforth by KRIBHCO in this direction has been acknowledged for three consecutive years by National Productivity Council by awarding first position to KRIBHCO for production, marketing and promotion of bio-fertilisers in the Nation.

CSR-CD PROGRAMMES AT NATIONAL LEVEL

NTPC will establish a foundation under Indian Trust Act 1882 for addressing the niche domains of social development at national level through strategic interventions. The NTPC Foundation will provide greater focus on identified issues of concern, create partnership with various stakeholders, receive funds from national and international agencies etc.

The Foundation will be the nodal agency for implementing the national level programmes as per the

CSR-CD policy of NTPC. The following niche domains of socio-economic development will be covered by the NTPC foundation.

a. To promote DDGS through covering the initial risks like cost of feasibility studies for the entrepreneur/ local communities,

b. To facilitate economic self- reliance of physically challenged persons, through establishing a development centre for physically challenged persons as national resource and development centre

c. To organise conservation of the national monuments and cultural heritage sites on selective basis

d. To provide relief and assistance during national calamities etc

e. To facilitate unemployed people in and around the new projects/ old stations in self-employment through co-operatives / self-help groups

f. Any other program/ activity related to social upliftment as deemed appropriate by he Foundation.

Aims and Objectives of NTPC Foundation

To facilitate the entrepreneurs/ communities in formulating the project proposals and establishing the feasibility for promoting the decentralized distributed generation and supply of power (DDGS) for meeting the power and development requirement of remote and far flung places. The foundation will consider the risk mitigation by bearing the cost of such feasibility studies where the project is found unviable. The foundation will also extend the NTPC's technical expertise in the field and provide the interface with NTPC – REC joint venture for collaboration and establishing DDGS as per the need and requirement.

The foundation will promote the plantation and forestry programmes for producing biomass required for DDGS programme. To facilitate the disabled persons in improving the economic and employment opportunities. For this, the foundation will establish an a development centre for physically challenged persons as national resource and development centre for enhancing the economic opportunities through strategic interventions such as

i. Extending cover for initial risks like conducting the feasibility studies, market research etc., in case the project is found un-viable.

ii. Facilitating micro-financing and/or venture/seed capital for project of economic self reliance and mentoring.

iii. Providing requisite support from initial phase of identification of livelihood opportunity till achieving the level of self sustenance.

iv. Conducting advocacy and awareness programs for identification of appropriate economic and employment opportunities

v. Identifying and administering the need based vocational/ managerial training programs with clear linkage to livelihood opportunity.

vi. Giving preference to small and medium projects covering a group of persons

To organise conservation of national monuments and cultural heritage sites on selective basis.

To provide appropriate assistance and send volunteers and resources for relief and restoration in the times of national calamities.

To facilitate the unemployed people in and around the new projects / old operating stations, in self-employment through co-operatives / self-help groups. The programme may include provisions for the enabling mechanism such as backward linkage like tying up the input resources and forward linkage like marketing etc. To take up or support any other social upliftment programme (in addition to the programmes stated above) at national level as deemed appropriate.

To develop and undertake advocacy, awareness campaigns and community outreach programmes in the above areas. To interact with policy makers, regulatory bodies and responding to issues initiated by them.

To organize workshops/ conferences/ symposia on the above areas and the related areas. To interact collaborate and promote partnership with other related national and international agencies/ organization and seek funds/ grants for specific programmes/ projects.

Institutional Set Up

NTPC Foundation: The NTPC Foundation will be governed by The Board of Trustees, details of which are given below:

CMD	Chairman of Board of Trustee
Dir (HR)	Trustee
Dir (Fin)	Trustee
Independent Director	Trustee

Professional with required experience and/ or with right aptitude and full commitment on an honorary basis Secretary to the Trust Or Director General

Staffing for Day to Day Operations: The professionals may be engaged on fixed term contract basis as program officers based on the need and requirement or volunteers from present and past NTPC employees may be deputed.

Development Centre for Physically Challenged Persons: The Development Centre for physically challenged persons will be a separate entity under the Foundation. The centre will be headed by a project director, who will report to the Board of the Trustees.

The Development Centre will address the following four categories of disability.

- Visually challenged persons
- Deaf and dumb persons
- Physically challenged persons
- Mentally challenged persons with mild intensity

The Development Centre will be located in its own building where, it will develop and maintain basic infrastructure facilities for providing supports like counselling, documentation centre, placement services, vocational training, market research etc. The Development Centre will also consider establishing sub-centres at regional / local level.

Implementation Mechanism

Planning & Co-ordination: The NTPC Foundation will be responsible for the overall planning and coordination of CD programmes at national level.

The Corporate CSR Group will coordinate with the NTPC Foundation for all related activities.

Monitoring and Evaluation: The monitoring of CD programme will be done by Foundation, which will submit quarterly report to NTPC management for its information.

The foundation will submit a quarterly progress report to the CSR group for apprising the management. The corporate CSR Group will review the work of Foundation and put up an exception report for appraising the management on quarterly basis. The details will be presented to NTPC Management on regular basis. The effectiveness of CD programme will be evaluated through external agencies for providing required feed back and inputs to formulate and improve the programmes in future.

SAIL is committed to the realm of social responsibility. The major activities in this field are briefly enumerated below.

HEALTH & MEDICAL

There are 20 state-of-the-art hospitals situated through out the country having a total strength of around 4500 beds for the benefit of employees, their dependants and the peripheral population and are managed by around 6000 doctors, medical and paramedical staff. SAIL has launched an AIDS Awareness and Control Program in partnership with National AIDS Control Organization [NACO], Ministry of Health & Family Welfare. Till date about Rs. 32 million have been received for implementing the policies of NACP-II in all Plants/Units.

PERIPHERAL DEVELOPMENT

Several socio-economic surveys reveal considerable benefits emanating from SAIL's efforts that reach interiors up to a radius of 8-15 kilometers. Programs are undertaken by each plant in close co-ordination with the State Government, District Administration as well as the local Panchayats, social organizations and people's representative of the area. Since the last 5 years the major plants have spent Rs. 10 million each in their allocated budget to carry out various programs every year.

EDUCATION

SAIL has continuously strived to provide the best of Education for the children and wards of employees. Over the years it has opened about 200 schools in the Steel Townships, which employ more than 6000 teachers who impart modern day education to over 1,00,000 children. Bhilai Steel Plant has adopted 36 tribal children of Chattisgarh region and is providing free education, boarding and lodging facilities.

SPORTS AND CULTURAL ACTIVITIES

SAIL has developed and nourished sports and games over a period of time and established *academies* for handball, hockey and football at Bhilai, Rourkela and Bokaro respectively. The handball and hockey academies are joint ventures with Sports Authority of India (SAI). As a result of the training, the academies are proud to have produced National, Commonwealth and SAF champions. SAIL has also given scholarships, amounting to Rs.4,200/- per annum, which have encouraged about 30 SAIL family children to either win national medals or be selected to the national teams.

Assistance During Natural Calamities

Employees of SAIL have always come forward to help and provide relief to the people affected by natural calamities such as floods, earthquakes etc. SAIL employees have given support in every possible form such as financial, relief materials, medical supplies, construction of houses & schools etc. in natural calamities which occurred in the recent past such as a severe earthquake in Jabalpur on 21/5/1997 and in Gujarat on 26/1/2001, cyclone floods at the eastern coast of Orissa in October 1999 and October 2001. In particular, relief material worth Rs. 1.00 crore was channelized through BSP on behalf of the entire SAIL collective in the 1999 cyclone flood in Orissa.

RASHTRIYA ISPAT NIGAM LIMITED (RINL)

Corporate Social Responsibility

In the year 2000, a universal code of practice for labour conditions in manufacturing industry was formulated under Social Accountability International (SAI) whose purpose was to develop voluntary standards for corporate social responsibility covering employees'working conditions to give a standard for socially responsible employment practices. Accordingly, the SA 8000 code of practice has been developed with nine key requirement areas, i.e. (i) Child Labour, (ii) Forced Labour (iii) health and Safety (iv) Freedom of association (v) Discrimination (vi) Disciplinary practices (vii) Working hours (viii) Compensation and (ix) Management.

All these have become statutes for the Indian Industries. RINL has been continuously shouldering social responsibility thorough various peripheral development activities. A separate cell on peripheral development is functional in the Town Administration department of the company. Initiatives for self sustenance of women and youth in and around VSP through training, employment generation schemes, etc. are undertaken on a continuous basis. Skill development programmes organised for various training programmes are also provided.

Till now, three villages have been adopted for development as model villages. Further, it has been planned to adopt at least one village every year with thrust on literacy, drinking water, health and hygiene. A committee has been constituted for planning and monitoring activities related to CSR. The top management also closely monitors the progress on various initiatives.

Summer Camps

Organising summer camps for school children during summer vacations is a regular feature. Yoga classes and coaching camps for various sports like cricket, badminton, volley ball, swimming, skating, etc. are also organised.

YOUTH HOSTELS ASSOCIATION

Youth hostels association of India, affiliated to International Youth Federation, functioning in VSP township, organises various knowledge exchange programmes and health camps. Health runs, cycle rallies, eye camps, pulse polio programmes, games and sports competitions are organised by this association.

NATIONAL MINERAL DEVELOPMENT CORPORATION (NMDC)

In all its Projects, NMDC has developed very good Townships with all amenities and infra-structural facilities like Schools, Hospitals, Community Cèntres, Market Places etc.

The Bailadila Projects are extending free medical facilities available in its Project hospitals to the local tribals. The Project Doctors with para-medical staff and medicines are regularly deputed to visit the interior villages to provide necessary medicare at the doorsteps of the tribals. The Company has also concentrated on providing potable drinking water by constructing tube wells as well as traditional open wells.

In order to ensure that the fruits of development are evenly distributed, NMDC has initiated a regular consultative process on the one hand with the local village- heads as well as Panchayat leaders and on the other hand with the Unions and Associations functioning in the Project. Periodical meetings are held with the Sarpanches of various tribal villages adjoining the Projects and tentative lists of the developmental works to be undertaken are detailed. Various Community/Peripheral development works undertaken by the company our Projects in and around their respective areas are as detailed below:-

Medicare: Free medical aid in all respects (both out-patient and in-patient), including Family Welfare counseling and operations including free diet is being provided to the Scheduled Tribes (Adivasis) residing within Dantewada

District in Project hospitals. Rest shelters have been provided for the use of family members of the Adivasi in- door patients. Health check-up programme has been instituted for the benefit of the primary school children in the surrounding villages. The company has active association in all eye camps, Pulse Polio immunization programmes/Family welfare camps organized by the District Administration for the benefit of the Adivasis and others within the District by deputing Project doctors/staff/vehicles.

Education: Free educational facilities for children of tribals (local adivasis) and Scheduled Caste students in Project Schools are provided. Besides constructing a number of school buildings, additional class rooms, ashrams and hostels, NMDC is regularly undertaking repair/renovation works to a number of school buildings of State Government and other Tribal schools in the vicinity of its Projects including electrification works.

Drinking Water

A number of hand pumps/Water Tanks/open wells/Tube wells have been constructed for supplying drinking water to the nearby villages. NMDC has also undertaken construction of overhead tanks in various areas for the benefit of local people, laying of pipeline to bring drinking water to different camps (labour camps, refugee camps etc.) away from the Project area, provision of drinking water to Degree college/ Schools and repairing of Public Health Engineering Dept's hand pumps and public utility water tanks.

Infrastructural Facilities

Following infrastructural development works have been undertaken by our Company:

a) Roads: All-weather Roads to a number of villages connecting one village and another - WBM roads from village to village, town to village etc. Construction/Improvement of approach roads to various villages - Black topping of PWD roads - Repairs to State highway.

b) Electrification work in the peripheral villages and various hamlets and provision of streetlights.

c) Provision of Steel Walkway Bridge over Madadi nallah.

Skill Development Programme

As a unique way of improving the competitiveness of middle pass local tribal youth every year, the Bailadila Projects introduced a 'Skill Development Programme' exposing them to various activities of the Projects. They are paid Rs.1200/- per month towards their out-of-pocket expenses in addition to providing them uniforms and other safety equipment. Regular classes are also held in order to improve their skill, performance and knowledge.

To enable the women folk of the villages to initiate self & community development works,Anganwadis were constructed in Hiroli, Prinar and Perpa villages - Bharat Matha Mahila Jagran Samiti, a voluntary organisation of women run by SCs/STs/OBCs employed in the NMDC and also from the adjoining villages, engaged in imparting training/coaching to womenfolk in sewing/adult literacy/ making household materials etc. has been provided suitable accommodation.

In the permanent community centers constructed by NMDC as well as in labour camps, cultural programmes/ weekly film shows are arranged for the entertainment and welfare of the employees and local population / adivasis. A primary Bailadila Adivasi & Harijan Unemployed Workers'Cooperative Society has been formed by the local youth with active cooperation from the Project. Since the Iron Ore Projects are situated in the heart of the tribal belt, a local market has been developed in the Project area, where Adivasis are encouraged to market their products in the *'Haat'*at Kirandul and Bacheli directly to the consumers. Special platforms with sheds and water facilities have been constructed for the exclusive use of Adivasis.. Over the years, the Bailadila Projects have also awarded contracts providing employment opportunities to adivasis for tree plantation in the Bailadila area to protect the environment and as a gesture of goodwill, employment to 43 local tribals from whom land was acquired. Upto 2001-02, the Bailadila Projects had spent around Rs.1600 lakhs on Community Development works. For the year 2002-03, various works were undertaken by NMDC in and around its Projects at a total cost of Rs.629.28 lakhs..

In other Projects of NMDC viz, Donimalai in Karnataka and Panna in MP such facilities are extended to the neighbouring villages under the 'Community Development Programme'. At Donimalai, two multipurpose Community Halls at the nearby villages have been constructed and handed over to the respective village Panchayats.

NMDC IRON AND STEEL PLANT, NAGARNAR, JAGADALPUR (CG)

NMDC is setting up an Iron and Steel plant near village Nagarnar in Bastar district of Chhatisgarh.

For construction of this plant, State Government of C.G. has acquired about 288.99 hectares of private land and allotted to NMDC apart from 114.01 hectares of Government land allotted by the Government of Chhatisgarh. NMDC has committed to make a comprehensive survey and implementation of a suitable scheme for total uplifment of the Cultural, Social, Economical, Educational and Health of the people residing in the Zone of influence of 10 KM around the plant in the state of Chattisgarh.

302 affected villagers have been given monetary compensation for their land and 98 persons whose total land was acquired have been provided suitable employment in the company's existing projects.

NMDC is also bearing the cost of training of any person of an affected family who gets admission in any ITI run by NMDC or recognized by the Government. Priority is being given to local cooperative societies in construction activities for supply of building materials etc.

KUDREMUKH IRON ORE COMPANY LIMITED

Kudremukh Iron Ore Company Limited has contributed immensely towards community development in and around the project. Some such developmental works are in the following areas:-

- Pure drinking water facilities.
- Play grounds, buildings, books and other financial assistance to the Educational Institutions.
- Development of social, cultural and recreation facilities.
- Health and Medical facilities.
- Assistance to the poor, disabled and downtrodden.
- Construction of buildings and provision of equipment to the hospitals.
- Construction of Bridges.
- Development of Coastal region.
- Rehabilitation.
- Supply of water for irrigation purposes.
- Construction of Irrigation Tank.
- Construction of a Panther Enclosure at Wild Life Safari of Pilikula Nisarga Dhama, Mangalore.

MANGANESE ORE(INDIA) LTD. (MOIL)

MOIL had adopted a tribal village viz Gondi, close to Ukwa Mines in Madhya Pradesh. The company has introduced a wide range of development activities such as repair of roads, construction of houses for homeless tribals, construction of school building to impart education to tribal children etc. as a part of their ongoing social welfare promotion scheme.

MOIL has about 7100 employees out of which more than 800 are women employees. As part of its Corporate Social responsibility, the Company is engaged in various welfare activities in and around its mining areas which include conducting medical camps, educational programmes, adoption of village and social forestry. The Company has taken up afforestation programmes towards maintenance of ecological balance in the mining areas. So far, MOIL has planted about 12 lakh saplings with a remarkable survival rate of over 80%.

SPONGE IRON INDIA LIMITED (SIIL)

SIIL continues to remain concerned about its social responsibilities besides the business goal it pursues. The Company's plant is located in a Scheduled Tribal Area predominantly having Schedules Castes/ Scheduled Tribes and backward population. The company has been giving priority to recruitment of personnel from these socially backward classes. Today at present out of the total employees strength of 322, 27% belongs to SC/ST and other backward classes.

SIIL has been carrying out its social obligation/ responsibilities towards not only its own employees and their families but also the population at large residing around the Plant and Township at Paloncha in Khammam District of Andhra Pradesh. Some of the activities being directly undertaken by the company and others where support is being provided by the company are:

a) Providing various facilities and infrastructural support to the employees and their families and local population like Chlorinated drinking water, Banking facilities, Post Office, LP Gas Outlet etc.

b) Major attention is focused on community health care by direct participation. This includes creating First Aid Centre, providing medical support to Tribal population in the nearby region, organizing medical camps such as Eye Camps, Anti-Leprosy Programme, Polio camps, AIDS and other health educational camps. Medicines are also provided free of cost to the Tribals and other weaker sections.

c) The company has been actively contributing towards spread of education in the region. It has also provided support in setting up of Primary standard to High School in its campus. The school is run with the assistance of private management efficiently and this is helping not only the children of employees of the company but also the local children. The school provides education both in English and Telugu medium.

d) The Company has been promoting awareness in maintaining the pollution free environment in and around its township and has also taken measures such as large scale tree plantation besides controlling its plant pollution through various measures. This continues to be an on-going activity. The General Manager (Works) of the Company is a member of the Environment control Committee of that area.

Considerable efforts have been made by the company and are being continued towards developing skilled personnel and vendors to meet the company's needs. This has resulted in setting up of small business units in and around Paloncha capable of providing various technical and other services to the company.

MECON LIMITED

MECON has been extensively associated with the rural/ community development activities since 60's. In the year 1976, a dedicated group was also formed and designated as Community Development Committee (CDC) to look after this activity.

The Community Development Committee of MECON has been working with the following objectives:-

a) Assist in harmonious development of the environment
b) Nurture communities towards optimum growth, so that they can become partners in progress
c) Concentrate on the poorest of the poor
d) Work together with NGO's & Government agencies towards common goals The activities being performed are briefly indicated below.

1. *Community Education Scheme:* Under this scheme, at present there are 12 primary/adult education centres for the poor in the slum areas/ rural areas/backward areas adopted village in an around Ranchi.
2. *Resource Generation Scheme:* Under the scheme, at present there are 7 resources generation centres, where the poor women are being trained.
3. *Vocational Training Institute:* The vocational training institute is affiliated to National Institute of Open Schooling, New Delhi. This was started in 1992 for providing technical education to poor and rural students. Presently, the institute offers three types of technical courses relating to Radio

& TV, Electrical and Welding technology. New courses on Computer Applications have also been started from the year 2003. Few other courses such as Refrigeration and Air Conditioning as well as Radiography are being planned and expected to be started shortly. This training is helping individuals to get jobs and also become self employed.

4. *Adopted Villages:* The company has adopted certain tribal villages and emphasis is given in the adopted villages on Community education schemes, Resources generation schemes, vocational training etc.
5. *Afforestation programme:* The company's horticulture department is distributing saplings and plants to the adopted villages as also to some of the parks, school, colleges and public places.
6. *Community medicine programme:* The community medicine programme includes general health check-ups, allopathic treatment, homeopathic treatment and specialized medical camps etc.
7. *Other welfare activities:* This includes an awareness programme for school children and villagers on computers, various other trades and other important aspects.

HINDUSTAN STEELWORKS CONSTRUCTION LIMITED (HSCL)

About 80% of the Company's employees and their families are stationed at SAIL/RINL Steel Plants – Bokaro, Bhilai and Vizag. These Units organized the following activities during 2003-04:

- Tree plantation in HSCL township
- Republic Day and Independence Day celebration

- Cultural functions on special days of National Importance.

BIRD GROUP OF COMPANIES

The Orissa Mineral Development Corporation (OMDC) under the group runs one 20 bedded hospital at Thakurani with Ambulance facility. Villagers from adjacent villages are allowed free treatment at the hospital. One Lady Medical Officer is attached to OMDC hospital for taking care of female patients.

The Bisra Stone Lime Co. Ltd (BSLC) runs one 40 bedded hospital at Birmitrapur with Ambulance facility. Villagers of adjacent villages are allowed treatment at this hospital on nominal charges. This hospital has a tie up with the Ispat General Hospital (IGH) of Rourkela Steel Plant at Rourkela for emergency cases.

Occupational health surveillance covering facilities like X-Ray, pathological laboratory, audiometry, ECG, Lungs function test, dental clinic, operation theatre etc is conducted by OMDC from time to time.

The RNTCP, Pulse Polio, Malaria eradication programme of the Government are also carried out through hospitals of OMDC and BSLC.

Drinking water is provided by dug wells, tube-wells etc. The Company also has a water lorry for supplying drinking water in the remote areas. Both OMDC and BSLC extend aid to peripheral schools and colleges in the form of construction of building, arranging study materials, providing furniture, school buses etc. The Companies actively participate in the TLC and also other Govt. IEC activities.

The companies also take up afforestation work at its mines for maintaining the ecological balance through active participation from the local villages.

JINDAL VIJAYANAGAR STEEL LIMITED(JVSL)

JVSL has initiated a large number of programs for integrated development of the society. The development needs and social initiatives are identified keeping in view changing life style and community needs. The major initiatives undertaken during the year 2003-2004 are as follows: -

a) JVSL has built a new township at Vijay Vittal Nagar consisting of 358 houses for its outsource employees which is the first of its kind in the industrial sector. Another 250 houses along with shopping complex, community hall and a temple are under construction.

b) As a part of promoting community health services a 22 bedded, fully air conditioned, Jindal Sanjeevani Hospital with secondary and tertiary health care services was established in July, 2004. Large number of free health checkup camps including cardiac assessment, ante natal clinics, tuberculosis detection, blood donation and immunization services for community children have been organised.

c) Vocation training centre for tailoring is being run for women, which offers one year Diploma course recognised by Government of Karnataka.

d) Organic framing has been popularized in two nearby villages, Vaddu and Kurekuppa for growing onions and other corps.

e) In association with Azim Premji Foundation, a Computer Assisted Learning Centre with an investment of Rs. 3.5 lakhs has been started for school children and training of primary school teachers. 40 teachers have been trained in this project.

f) A hundred years old school, Chatrapati Shivaji School at Sandur has been renovated with play grounds for Basket ball, Football and other facilities.

g) 1.4 km of cement road in Sandur has been constructed.

SESA GOA GROUP OF COMPANIES

Peripheral development: Sesa Goa commenced broad based community and social development programmes in early 1960's, initially by providing drinking water to surrounding villages and conducting in-house training for local youth in the maintenance and operation of mine machinery, thus providing gainful employment. Other programmes soon followed including community health, first aid and ambulance coverage for local communities.

The Company has undertaken a participatory approach with the community to rejenuviate the abandoned and marginal paddy fields, to its original health. Three years joint efforts have led to a sustainable bumper paddy crop to the farmers. Eventually, it was decided to formalize the Company's community development programmes. Accordingly a socio economic study of the surrounding communities was undertaken through a reputed institute at the cost of Rs 1.5 million. The study helped to identify community expectations and help meet basic developmental needs.

Sesa Goa also established the SESA COMMUNITY DEVELOPMENT FOUNDATION in 1996 to further its social activities and meet its responsibilities. Under this initiative, the Sesa Technical School and Sesa Goa Football Academy have been established which provide technical education and football coaching to young local youth.

Sesa Technical School was established to provide technical education to children of surrounding villages. In the school, technical training is provided in five trades i.e. Fitter, Welder, Mechanics, Draughtsman, and Electrical. The prime objective of the school is to train local youth in employment oriented fields so as to enhance their opportunities of securing employment, in industry. Sesa Football Academy was established with an initial capital of

Rs 80 lakhs and an annual budget of 30 lakhs. The academy is residential with 30 trainers accommodated for a four-year programme. The trainees are provided with formal education apart from professional training in football. The students passing out from the academy have been well received by the professional clubs at National Level. Sesa Goa is a founder member and major contributor to the "Mineral Foundation of Goa". The foundation is formed by the Mineral Industry in Goa to undertake social and environmental related programmes.

Trade Shows

Trade shows are events at which companies display their wares to customers and potential customers. They are thus useful for gathering intelligence about a company's marketing plans. Some corporate campaigners also find them useful opportunities to put public pressure on a company. To learn about upcoming trade shows at which your target company may exhibit, try TSNN or ExhibitorNet.

Exports and Imports

The best source of data on international shipment of goods is an expensive service called PIERS (Port Import/Export Reporting Services), which is available online directly from the company or via Lexis-Nexis.

ANALYZING A COMPANY'S SOCIAL RESPONSIBILITY RECORD

Companies also have relationships with their employees and with the communities in which they do business. The way they conduct these relationships is known as the company's social responsibility record. All too many companies behave in an irresponsible manner—breaking the law, violating regulations, mistreating workers, despoiling the environment and manipulating public policy through lobbying and campaign contributions. Investigating these issues is an essential part of any thorough corporate research project.

SOCIAL RESPONSIBILITY PROFILES AND RATINGS; DISSIDENT WEBSITES

The social investing movement has grown in size and sophistication over the past two decades. One of the outcomes of this is that several organizations provide useful profiles of the social responsibility record of large companies. Some of these sources tend to be weak on labor relations issues, but they have good information on other employment matters (affirmative action, etc.), environmental issues and so forth. Among these are:

- SocialFunds.com has a section called the Corporate Social Research Center that provides links to social responsibility information on hundreds of companies.
- Co-Op America has a site called Responsible Shopper that rates about 350 consumer products companies according to workplace, environmental and disclosure issues.
- A website called Idealswork combines information on the social responsibility record of consumer companies with a shopping resource. Idealswork gives a portion of its commission on the sales to non-profits.
- KLD Research & Analytics has what is perhaps the most comprehensive database of social responsibility profiles. Unfortunately, the service, called SOCRATES, is aimed at institutional investors and is thus very expensive. For more information, see KLD's site.

For current news about corporate misdeeds, one of the best (but expensive) sources is the weekly *Corporate Crime Reporter*.

Another source of information on the business practices of companies, including very small ones, is the Better Business Bureau, which has been collecting consumer complaints since 1912. The Bureau has a website that contains a search engine through which you can research the reputation of business establishments (at least as measured by the number of customer complaints) throughout the country.

Dissident Websites

Another source of critical (though not always accurate) information on companies are websites that have been created by people who have a grievance against the firm, who disagree with its policies, or who just don't like it. See, for example, Jiffy Lube Sucks and I Hate Starbucks. It has also become common for unions or environmental groups that are engaged in a corporate campaign against a company to create such a site. Use a general search engine such as Google to find such sites on your target company.

COURT PROCEEDINGS

Investigating a company's involvement in litigation is useful for two reasons. First, it says something about a firm's way of operating if it frequently ends up as a defendant in lawsuits over matters such as race and sex discrimination, defective products and antitrust violations – not to mention outright fraud. Second, in the course of legal proceedings, companies will often be required to divulge information that might otherwise never make it into the public domain. The latter is also true in court proceedings—especially divorces—involving a top executive or owner of your target company.

The place to begin, if you are dealing with a public company, is the 10-K filing (see above), which contains a section called Legal Proceedings. Companies are supposed to use this section to describe any legal matters that could have a material impact on the firm's finances. Some companies choose to interpret this narrowly and say little or nothing about litigation; other firms may provide a long narrative of legal issues.

The 10-K is just a starting point, so you need how to do an independent litigation search. There are four main types of court information that you can access:

Dockets

These are lists of pending and recently closed cases that contain basic information about the nature of the case, the parties involved and a chronology of events (motions, rulings, etc.) in the case. Until a few years ago, the only way to search dockets was to go to the courthouse where the case was filed. Today nearly all federal courts and a growing number of state courts have put their dockets online.

The dockets of federal district, appellate and bankruptcy courts can be accessed through a fee-based system called PACER (Public Access to Court Electronic Records), which is run by the Administrative Office of the U.S. Courts. In order to use the system you must open an account and pay a modest fee based on usage. In addition to providing access to individual courts, PACER provides access to the U.S. Party/Case Index, which allows you to search most, but not all federal court dockets at once for cases in which a specific company or individual is a party.

Courtlink, a commercial service owned by Lexis-Nexis, provides a more convenient and speedier system for accessing PACER information, though at a substantially higher price. Westlaw also provides access to PACER docket information.

The U.S. Tax Court, which hears cases brought by companies and individuals challenging IRS notices of deficiency, puts its docket online. Tax Court cases are important to check, because they may require a company to put its tax return into the public record.

State courts have been somewhat slower in putting their dockets online, but they are starting to catch up. For a list of which courts are available electronically, check LLRX.com. Courtlink also provides access to some state court dockets. If you do a large amount of docket checking, you may want to subscribe to a pay website called Legal Dockets Online, which provides a comprehensive set of links to PACER and state court sites.

Court Filings

Once your docket search has turned up an interesting case, the way to find out more about the matter is to look at the actual documents that have been filed by the parties. These would include things such as the original complaint (in a civil matter) or indictment (in a criminal matter), briefs, motions, depositions and transcripts of court proceedings. Generally speaking, these documents are available only in hard-copy form at the clerk's office of the court in which the case was filed.

The federal courts, however, have been developing an extension of PACER that allows subscribers to view images of court filings on their home or office computer. The list of links to court sites on the PACER Service Center site indicates which ones have begun to post document images. Legal Dockets Online (see above) also has this information.

Verdicts, Judgments and Liens

There are a variety of reporting services around the country that collect information about significant verdicts in civil cases. There are also some that collect nationwide data. For example, the *National Law Journal* has a pay site called VerdictSearch. A number of services are collected in the Verdicts Library on Lexis-Nexis and on Westlaw.

Financial judgments in civil matters become a matter of public record as do liens on property and federal and state tax liens. You can search these records at the county courthouse in the jurisdiction where the action occurred. If you want to do a wider search, use services such as KnowX, the Liens Library on Lexis-Nexis or Westlaw.

Written Opinions

Lawyers and legal researchers review written opinions via expensive services such as Lexis-Nexis or Westlaw. Both allow you to search for cases in which a particular company was a party and to display the full text of the opinions. At the federal level, more and more courts are putting their opinions on the web. See the websites of individual courts; for a list of links, see the Federal Judiciary site or Legal Dockets Online (see above).

Legal Representation

To find out which law firms are used by the 250 largest companies in the United States, see the annual list called Who Defends Corporate America, which is published by the *National Law Journal*. The list can be found online (click on Legal Surveys). Determining which law firms list a particular company as a client can also be done by searching the electronic version of the Martindale-Hubbell directory on Lexis-Nexis.

FEDERAL REGULATORY MATTERS

The Securities and Exchange Commission

The SEC, which regulates publicly traded companies as well as entities and individuals involved in the securities industry, has been much in the news because of controversy over its failure to prevent or even detect the spate of corporate financial scandals in recent years. The SEC does, however, engage in enforcement. The agency's website contains an archive of Litigation Releases dating back to September 1995; Lexis-Nexis has an archive that goes back decades.

The SEC site also has information about administrative proceedings of its Division on Enforcement. Also check out the Securities Class Action Clearinghouse for information on fraud lawsuits brought on behalf of investors against public companies.

Federal Trade Commission

The FTC enforces a variety of consumer protection laws and shares enforcement of the antitrust laws with the Department of Justice. The Commission's website contains an archive of formal opinions it has taken since 1996. The Trade Library on Lexis-Nexis has an archive of consent decrees that companies have signed with the FTC since 1980. It also has an archive of Justice Department final judgments during that same period.

Federal Product Regulators

The Consumer Product Safety Commission has an archive of product recalls and other commission actions. The Food and Drug Administration has an archive of safety alerts and product recalls. The National Highway Traffic Safety Administration has an archive of motor vehicle recalls.

For more on product safety, see the website of the non-profit Underwriters Laboratories, which includes a database of which products it has certified.

General Services Administration

The GSA, which oversees federal purchasing, maintains a list of those individuals and companies that have been barred from doing business with the federal government for violations of various kinds; it is called the Excluded Parties Listing System.

See also the Federal Contractor Misconduct Database, which is assembled by the Project On Government Oversight.

See below for information relating to the Environmental Protection Agency, the Federal Election Commission and the Occupational Safety and Health Administration.

LABOR RELATIONS AND EMPLOYMENT PRACTICES

Public company 10-K filings (see above) contain a section indicating the number of employees and the portion of the workforce covered by collective bargaining agreements. Companies that deal with unions to a significant extent may also name the unions, indicate how many employees are members and give a description of the general state of labor relations. In almost all cases, the company will say that those relations are good.

On the other hand, there is substantial evidence that this country's low level of unionization is in large part a result of anti-union animus on the part of many employers. A key way to document a company's labor relations record is to look at the unfair labor practice (ULP) charges that have been filed against it by unions or individual workers.

The website of the National Labor Relations Board has an archive of the agency's written decisions going back to 1984. To do a comprehensive search of ULPs that may have been filed against a company, as well as other aspects of a firm's labor practices, the best source is the Labor Database CD-ROM compiled by the Food and Allied Service Trades Department of the AFL-CIO. Among its contents are:

- an index of all ULPs since 1990;
- data on NLRB elections since 1990;
- data on collective bargaining agreements filed with the Federal Mediation and Conciliation Service since 1990;
- compliance data since 1996 relating to the Fair Labor Standards Act (overtime, minimum wage and child

labor violations), Davis-Bacon and Service Contract Act (prevailing wage violations); the Family Medical Leave Act and other employment laws; and

- Equal Employment Opportunity Commission cases since 1989.

For information on ordering the CD, see the FAST website.

The AFL-CIO has a database called UNICORE that contains extensive data showing which companies have relationships with which unions. Requests to access the database must usually come through an international union. If you need to know which unions a (large) company deals with but you cannot get access to UNICORE, some of that information can be found in a volume called *Profiles of American Labor Unions,* which was last published by the Gale Group in 1998. The AFL-CIO's Union Label and Service Trades Department also has a list of union-made products and services.

The AFL also has a site (to which trade unionists can get a password) called Bust the Union Busters. It contains information on the use of anti-union law firms and consultants and can be searched by company name. Similar information is openly available on the website of American Rights at Work, especially the sections on The Anti-Union Network. The AFL-CIO National Boycott List of anti-union companies can be found on the web.

A website called FreeErisa has information on labor relations as well as employee benefits. Its features include:

- Results of NLRB elections and ULP cases by company;
- A list of companies that are parties to collective bargaining agreements on file with the U.S. Bureau of Labor Statistics (this information is also available directly from on the BLS website);

- Data contained in Form 5500 filings that companies have to make to the U.S. Department of Labor about their employee benefit plans.

Decisions of U.S. Department of Labor Administrative Law Judges on cases involving matters such as black lung claims, ERISA disputes and whistleblower cases can be found here.

DOL also has a disclosure page with information on foreign labor certifications (including pay levels) given to companies that claim they have to import foreign workers to the United States to perform certain jobs.

The best news sources on U.S. labor relations are publications of the Bureau of National Affairs: the *Daily Labor Report* and *Labor Relations Week*. If you subscribe to these expensive publications online, you can search for past articles that mention your target company. The BNA newsletters are also available on Lexis-Nexis and Westlaw.

Foreign Sweatshops

In recent years, more and more information has come to light about the dismal working conditions of third world factories that supply multinational corporations. Here are some sources for information about sweatshops:

- National Labor Committee
- Sweatshop Watch
- United Students Against Sweatshops

WORKPLACE SAFETY AND HEALTH

Health and safety conditions on the job have been a matter of public controversy since the beginning of the Industrial Revolution. For the past three decades in the United States, those conditions have been regulated by a federal agency, the Labor Department's Occupational Safety and Health Administration. To carry out its mandate, OSHA is supposed to conduct periodic inspections of workplaces and cite employers for any violations that are found. The OSHA website has a database that contains the results of every inspection the agency has carried out since 1972.

The Mine Safety and Health Administration's Data Retrieval System contains accident and violation histories for specific mines as well as inspection dust sampling data.

ENVIRONMENTAL COMPLIANCE

One of the ways in which many companies fail to act in a socially responsible manner is by violating environmental regulations, which all too many corporate executives regard as an annoyance rather than a means of protecting public health. Environmental regulation in the United States is conducted both at the federal level – through the Environmental Protection Agency (EPA) – and at the state level. The EPA website is a source of a great deal of data on environmental matters. Start at the Envirofacts page, which allows you to search a variety of EPA databases at once for data on a particular geographic location. If you enter the zip code of a facility of your target company, Envirofacts will give you information such as the following:

- data on your target facility and others located in the same zip code that produce air pollution (from Aerometric Information Retrieval System)
- data on toxics (from the Toxics Release Inventory)
- data on hazardous waste (from the Resource Conservation and Recovery Act database and from the Superfund list of the worst hazardous waste sites)
- data on water quality (from the National Drinking Water Contaminant Occurrence Database and the Permit Compliance System).

Envirofacts also has a feature that maps much of this information. Environmental Defense has a valuable site that combines data from the Envirofacts databases and other sources to give a comprehensive profile of the environmental condition of a given location.

In 2002 the EPA made a major advance in disclosure with the launch of a pilot website containing enforcement data on some 800,000 regulated facilities nationwide. The service, called Enforcement and Compliance History Online (ECHO), contains information relating to Clean Air Act stationary sources, Clean Water Act facilities with direct discharge permits (under the National Pollutant Discharge Elimination System), and generators/handlers of hazardous waste regulated under the Resource Conservation and Recovery Act. It also provides information on state enforcement data.

A page of links to state environmental agencies can be found on the Clay.net site. For links to environmental groups working in various areas, see the Environmental Organization Web Directory.

CAMPAIGN CONTRIBUTIONS AND LOBBYING

Corporations are barred from making direct contributions to federal candidates, but they do find other ways to greatly influence the political process. These include individual contributions by company executives, contributions through company Political Action Committees (PACs) and company contributions to political parties. The latter, known as soft money contributions, have been outlawed by federal campaign reform legislation (though it appears companies are finding ways around the restrictions).

These various kinds of contributions are part of the public record and are disclosed via reports issued by the Federal Election Commission. The FEC website has a database with lists of contributions and files with images of the original documents.

Several organizations have taken the FEC data and created websites with extensive analysis and better searching capabilities. Among the best of these is the Center for Responsive Politics site, which contains, for example, excellent analyses of contribution patterns by industries and interest groups. FECInfo's Political Money Line has more extensive historical data, but you have to pay a subscription fee to access all of its features.

State contribution data has been slower to come on line, but the Institute on Money in State Politics has done a heroic job in gathering the information and putting it in a uniform searchable format. The Institute's site allows for searches by contributor or recipient in specific states or across the entire country. For some states the information starts as early as 1990. Note that some states allow direct campaign contributions by corporations.

For access to the personal financial disclosure forms filed by members of Congress and top federal officials, see the site compiled by the Center for Responsive Politics.

Lobbying

Federal lobbyists have to submit semi-annual reports to the Secretary of the Senate and the Clerk of the House identifying their clients and the amount of income they receive. Companies have to report their overall lobbying expenditures and the names of any lobbyists employed as part of an in-house lobbying effort. The Senate has put its filings online in a database that allows you to search by the name of the client. Political Money Line has a page that provides access to the lobbyist disclosure forms by industry. A good compilation of available data can be found on the Lobbying Spending Database created by the Center for

Responsive Politics. For lists of which lobbyists represent a given company, you can also consult the print volumes *Washington Representatives* (which is published by Columbia Books and is also available through a pay website) and the *Government Affairs Yellow Book* (which is published by Leadership Directories and is also available along with other directories on a CD-ROM or a subscription website).

State websites contain a list of the lobbyists registered in the legislature.

PUBLIC RELATIONS, CORPORATE PHILANTHROPY AND SPONSORED RESEARCH

Public relations is essentially a process of lobbying the public, either directly or through the media. Large companies spend large amounts of money to build their image. Think, for example, of the ad campaigns that the likes of tobacco maker Philip Morris and Wal-Mart have conducted to publicize corporate disaster relief efforts.

Companies use both in-house personnel and outside public relations agencies to carry out these initiatives. *The National Directory of Corporate Public Affairs*, published by Columbia Books, is the best collection of information on corporate flacks. See also *O'Dwyers Directory of Public Relations Firms*, published by J.R. O'Dwyer & Co., which also provides data online. To keep up with trends in corporate propaganda, subscribe to the newsletter *PR Watch*; the website also includes profiles of industry front groups. For information on which companies are sponsoring which events, see Sponsorship.com.

One of the more aggressive forms of p.r. is manipulation of scientific research. For information on industry ties to scientists and non-profits, see the Center for Science in the Public Interest database. Charitable contributions are one of the ways that companies do public relations. Sometimes companies set up their own foundations to conduct this activity. For larger companies, check the website to see if there is a report on philanthropic activities. The *Corporate Giving Directory*, published by the Taft Group, has data on direct contributions by companies. The Foundation Center, whose website is the best online source of information on corporate and other foundations, publishes the *National Directory of Corporate Giving* and *Corporate Foundation Profiles*. A newer resource is NOZA, a database that assembles details of charitable contributions by individuals as well as companies.

Private foundations, like other non-profits, must file a Form 990 with the Internal Revenue Service (the private foundation version is called the 990-PF). These documents, which are public records, contain a great deal of information about the finances of the foundation and usually contain a list of the organizations that have received grants. Scanned images of 990s can be accessed on the web at Guidestar.

Some states also regulate charities and may have reporting requirements in addition to the 990. For a list of links to such states, see the Portico site.

EXECUTIVE COMPENSATION

Excessive pay for top corporate executives is a perennial problem in corporate America. Finding out how much CEOs and other top dogs in publicly traded companies earn is not difficult. The information – including stock option data – is spelled out down to the dollar in the company's proxy statement (Form DEF 14A), which can be obtained online through the EDGAR system (see above). For faster access to summary compensation information on a company, use the website eComp. For more on the subject of executive compensation, see the AFL-CIO's Executive Paywatch site and United for a Fair Economy.

GOVERNMENT SUBSIDIES

Over the past few decades, corporate executives have come to expect that government will subsidize their operations in one way or another. The federal tax code and the tax policies of the states provide a myriad of subsidies for particular types of companies or business in general. Yet there are also programs that provide individual companies with special tax abatements/exemptions or direct grants, loans or loan guarantees. These benefits, often called corporate welfare, are usually justified in the name of economic growth or development.

At the federal level, there are several programs that promote U.S. exports or foreign investment by U.S. companies:

- The Commerce Department's Advanced Technology Program, which funds corporate research. The program's website has a list of funded projects.
- The Export-Import Bank, which provides loans and loan guarantees to promote sales of U.S. goods to overseas buyers. Its website has an archive of annual reports that list sellers and buyers.
- The Overseas Private Investment Corporation, which provides political research insurance. OPIC's website does not have a database of clients, but the site does archive press releases and annual reports that list companies receiving OPIC aid.
- Some companies are recipients of farm subsidies offered through the U.S. Department of Agriculture. A database of recipients of such subsidies has been compiled by the Environmental Working Group.

Cities and states offer subsidies to companies to induce them to move their headquarters or locate a factory or other facility in a given jurisdiction. There is no central database of these handouts; in fact, only a small number of states have laws requiring that economic development subsidies be disclosed. The public may learn about the subsidies only when politicians in the community that won the contest brag to the media about how they lured a new job-creating facility. Unions or community groups that want to know the details of the subsidies often have to file a freedom of information request—and even then may be denied the documents on the grounds that they contain proprietary information.

The one area in which better disclosure exists is in connection with Industrial Development Bonds (also known as Industrial Revenue Bonds). State and local governments issue these IDBs on behalf of manufacturing companies to help finance new factories or other facilities. The company is responsible for payments to bondholders, but the interest on IDBs is exempt from federal (and often state) income tax. For this reason, the bonds can offer significantly lower interest rates than regular corporate bonds, which makes the bonds an appealing source of low-cost financing. For more on tax-exempt bonds, see a website called Public Bonds.

When IDBs are offered to the public, the company has to prepare a prospectus known as an Official Statement. The OS will contain information about the planned facility and the company itself, which may include financial data about privately held as well as public companies. Because private companies generally do not want to reveal much about their finances, they will often take advantage of a loophole in the law that allows IDB issuers that have a bank letter of credit to forgo financial disclosure.

4

Business Development

Business development includes a number of techniques designed to create and grow an economic enterprise. Such techniques include, but are not limited to, concept and brand development, assessment of marketing opportunities and target markets, intelligence gathering on customers and competitors, generating leads for possible sales, followup sales activity, formal proposal writing and business model design. Business development involves evaluating a business and then realizing its full potential, using such tools as marketing, sales, information management and customer service. For a sound company able to withstand competitors, business development never stops but is an ongoing process.

Successful business development often requires a multi-disciplinary approach beyond just "a sale to a customer." A detailed strategy for growing the business in desirable ways is frequently necessary, which may involve financial, legal and advertising skills. Business development cannot be reduced to simple templates applicable to all or even most situations faced by real-world enterprises. Creativity in meeting new and unforeseen challenges is necessary to keep an enterprise on a path of sustainable growth.

Small to medium-sized companies often do not establish procedures for business development, instead relying on their existing contacts. Other times they assume that because they know people in high places that their business development problems are solved and that somehow new business will come to them. The ramifications of such thinking can be significant in the event they are unable to leverage those relationships, which very often are personal or weak. Then they will have no new business in the pipeline.

Business development professionals are frequently found to have earlier careers in financial services/investment banking or management consulting; although many find their route by climbing the corporate ladder in functions such as operations management or sales.

The pipeline refers to flow of potential clients whom the company is in the process of developing. Each potential client in the pipeline is given a percent chance of success with projected sales volumes attached. The weighted average of all the potential clients in the pipeline can be used for staffing to manage the new business when it comes in

For larger and more well-established companies, especially in technology-related industries, business development often refers to creating and managing strategic relationships and alliances with other, third party companies. In these instances the companies will leverage one anothers' expertise, technologies or other intellectual property to expand their products, services, functionality and/or market reach without having to invest in building or acquiring these with internal resources. Revenues are typically shared in some sort of royalty arrangement. For example, a company with a successful technology will partner with a company that has an existing customer base and sales force, and together they will penetrate that market, sharing the proceeds.

The set of efforts for identifying, researching, analyzing and bringing to market new businesses and new products, business development focuses on implementation of the strategic business plan through equity financing, acquisition/

divestiture of technologies, products, and companies, plus the establishment of strategic partnerships where appropriate.

The Business Development Strategy is used to underpin your main Business Plan and essentially it sets out a standard approach for developing new opportunities, either from within existing accounts or by proactively targeting brand new potential accounts and then working to close them.

This document highlights the key issues you should consider prior to compiling your own plan and will hopefully guide you logically through a proven framework.

The key word is 'Strategy', because you are creating a workable and achievable set of objectives in order to exceed your annual target.

Your Starting Point:

The key words are Who? What? Where? When? Which? Why? How?

For example:

Who - are you going to target?

What - do you want to sell them?

Where - are they located?

When - will you approach them?

Which - are the appropriate target personnel?

Why - would they want to meet with you?

How - will you reach them?

If you have conducted regular account reviews with your key accounts during the previous twelve months, you should be aware of any new opportunities that will surface during the next twelve months. You will also, when assessing what percentage of your annual target usually comes from existing accounts, need to review data over the last two or three years. (It is likely that you can apply Pareto i.e. 80% of your business will probably come from existing accounts and in fact 80% of your total revenue will come from just 20% of your customers/clients)

You will be left with a balance - i.e. "20% of my business next year will come from new opportunities" - therefore you can then begin to allocate your selling time accordingly.

Ideal Customer Profiling: Pro-active business development demands that we create an ideal target at the front end - i.e. an Ideal Customer Profile. The essential characteristics you will need to consider are:

- Industrial Sector
- Geographical Location (Demographics)
- Size of organisations (Turnover, number of employees etc)
- Financial Trends
- Psychographics - i.e. Philosophical compatibility

Many strategic sales professionals merely profile their best existing clients and try to replicate them - there's nothing wrong with doing this but we should always remember that we are seeking an IDEAL and we can always improve on what we already have.

'New' Opportunities From Within 'Old' Accounts: Because it costs approximately ten times as much, to first locate and then sell to a new customer as it does an existing one (although these costs are rarely reflected in the cost of sales), it is essential that we fully develop our existing accounts working upwards, downwards and sideways, thus making the most of the (hopefully) excellent reputation we have developed already.

Most corporate accounts have several divisions, departments, sites, even country offices and you must satisfy yourself that you have exhausted every possible avenue. Don't be afraid to ask the question "Who else should I be talking to in your organisation"?

Developing New Opportunities: There are a number of ways in which we can target new opportunities e.g.

- Direct Mail
- Telephone Canvassing
- Researching Archived Files For Customers Who Used To Buy From Your Company
- Exhibitions
- Seminars
- User Groups
- E-Mail Campaigns
- Referrals
- Qualified Leads
- Advertising

Not all of these will be appropriate to your particular industry, but you should not be afraid to experiment - i.e. challenge the paradigm - and do not accept that just because a particular idea has not worked in the past that it will not do so in the future. (Remember when you were learning to walk - it didn't work first time then!)

The important thing is to make an early decision in terms of what you are going to try and then build this (those) ideas into your master plan.

A Typical Business Development Plan: You should plan out the whole year and review / revise quarterly.

- List your existing accounts and plan what activities / actions need to be completed in order to fully exhaust all opportunities. You may for instance, plan to cover more bases within the decision making unit or contact associated companies or offices. The Strategic Account Profile can be used as a prompt.

- Begin to target new accounts using business directories etc. and set targets per week / month / quarter i.e. I normally allow for eight hours per week as a minimum (Don't forget to continually refer back to your Ideal Profile)
- Then build in what assistance you need from your marketing function - i.e. qualified leads, seminars, exhibition attendance etc.
- Finally share your plan with your manager and then commit to it.

You should also measure it against S.M.A.R.T.E.R. i.e. is it.

S.pecific

M.easurable

A.chievable

R.elevant

T.imed

E.xciting

R.ecorded

Linking With Your Commercial Plan: I have suggested that your Business Development Strategy, would link with your Master Business Plan but logically you should also integrate it into your Commercial Kit(this is a document that outlines your monthly,quarterly and annual targets) - specifically the areas that deal with new business generation, account management and development, four tier account lists etc.

These three documents when combined should drive and guide you through the next twelve months and beyond.

Summary: As I have said often enough "People do not fail because they planned to fail but rather because they failed to plan"

The man who knows where he wants to go is more likely to get there, he just has to decide how to get there. All plans are essentially maps and guides; the strategic element is the 'How'.

Do be prepared to change course, flexibility is key, and don't be afraid to experiment, look outside the square.

BUSINESS STRATEGIES FOR SUSTAINABLE DEVELOPMENT

Based on the book *Business Strategy for Sustainable Development: Leadership and Accountability for the* ***90s***, published in 1992 by the International Institute for Sustainable Development in conjunction with Deloitte & Touche and the World Business Council for Sustainable Development.

The concept of sustainable development has received growing recognition, but it is a new idea for many business executives. For most, the concept remains abstract and theoretical.

Protecting an organization's capital base is a well-accepted business principle. Yet organizations do not generally recognize the possibility of extending this notion to the world's natural and human resources.

If sustainable development is to achieve its potential, it must be integrated into the planning and measurement systems of business enterprises. And for that to happen, the concept must be articulated in terms that are familiar to business leaders. The following definition is suggested:

For the business enterprise, sustainable development means adopting business strategies and activities that meet the needs of the enterprise and its stakeholders today while protecting, sustaining and enhancing the human and natural resources that will be needed in the future.

This definition captures the spirit of the concept as originally proposed by the World Commission on Environment and Development, and recognizes that economic development must meet the needs of a business enterprise and its stakeholders. The latter include shareholders, lenders, customers, employees, suppliers and communities who are affected by the organization's activities.

It also highlights business's dependence on human and natural resources, in addition to physical and financial capital. It emphasizes that economic activity must not irreparably degrade or destroy these natural and human resources.

This definition is intended to help business directors apply the concept of sustainable development to their own organizations. However, it is important to emphasize that sustainable development cannot be achieved by a single enterprise (or, for that matter, by the entire business community) in isolation. Sustainable development is a pervasive philosophy to which every participant in the global economy (including consumers and government) must subscribe, if we are to meet today's needs without compromising the ability of future generations to meet their own.

IMPLICATIONS FOR BUSINESS

It has become a cliché that environmental problems are substantial, and that economic growth contributes to them. A common response is stricter environmental regulation, which often inhibits growth. The result can be a trade-off between a healthy environment on the one hand and healthy growth on the other. As a consequence, opportunities for business may be constrained.

However, there are some forms of development that are both environmentally and socially sustainable. They lead not to a trade-off but to an improved environment, together with development that does not draw down our environmental capital. This is what sustainable development is all about - a revolutionary change in the way we approach these issues.

Businesses and societies can find approaches that will move towards all three goals - environmental protection, social wellbeing and economic development - at the same time. Sustainable development is good business in itself. It creates opportunities for suppliers of 'green consumers', developers of environmentally safer materials and processes, firms that invest in eco-efficiency, and those that engage themselves in social well-being. These enterprises will generally have a competitive advantage. They will earn their local community's goodwill and see their efforts reflected in the bottom line.

PRACTICAL CONSIDERATIONS

While business traditionally seeks precision and practicality as the basis for its planning efforts, sustainable development is a concept that is not amenable to simple and universal definition. It is fluid, and changes over time in response to increased information and society's evolving priorities.

The role of business in contributing to sustainable development remains indefinite. While all business enterprises can make a contribution towards its attainment, the ability to make a difference varies by sector and organization size.

Some executives consider the principal objective of business to be making money. Others recognize a broader social role. There is no consensus among business leaders as to the best balance between narrow self-interest and actions taken for the good of society. Companies continually face the need to trade off what they would 'like' to do and what they 'must' do in pursuit of financial survival.

Businesses also face trade-offs when dealing with the transition to sustainable practices. For example, a chemical company whose plant has excessive effluent discharges might decide to replace it with a more effective treatment facility. But should the company close the existing plant during the two or three-year construction period and risk losing market share? Or should it continue to operate the polluting plant despite the cost of fines and adverse public relations? Which is the better course of action in terms of economy, social wellbeing and the environment?

Moreover, many areas of sustainable development remain technically ambiguous, making it difficult to plan an effective course of action. For example, the forestry industry has had difficulty defining what constitutes sustainable forest management. Some critics believe that simply replacing trees is not enough, because harvesting destroys the biodiversity of the forest. Clearly, more research will be needed to resolve such technical issues.

From a broader perspective, however, it is clearly in the interest of business to operate within a healthy environment and economy. It is equally plain that, on a global basis, growing and sustainable economies in the developing countries will provide the best opportunities for expanding markets.

To some, sustainable development and environmental stewardship are synonymous. In the short term, sound environmental performance is probably a reasonable objective for most businesses, with sustainable development as a longer term goal. However, this can lead to confusion. In the developed world, the focus is on environmental management, while in developing countries, rapid and sustainable development is paramount. The global economy is coming under growing pressure to pay for the restoration of damaged environments. But this economic engine is being asked to help solve other pressing problems at the same time. The challenge is to solve all of these problems in a sustainable manner, so as to generate continuing development.

Despite ambiguities about definitions, there is now widespread support for sustainable development principles within the business community. However, for that support to grow, it will be important to recognize and reward initiatives that are being taken to turn the concept into reality.

POSITIVE SIGNS OF CHANGE

William Mulligan, environmental affairs manager at Chevron Corporation, reflects the view of many in the business community who believe that the environment is now a major issue - one which presents both challenges and opportunities. 'Over the last decade, we have seen many polls confirming the importance of the environment to Americans,' he says.

'Only an irresponsible company would dismiss this trend as a passing fad or fail to recognize the need to integrate environmental considerations into every aspect of its business. Environmental excellence has to become part of strategic thinking. It is in our best economic interests to do so. In fact, whenever we are forced to change, we often find opportunities.'

This positive change in attitudes and practices is echoed by the Organization for Economic Cooperation and Development, which says: 'There is now a realistic prospect of harmonizing environmental and economic considerations, and thus of gradually incorporating these objectives in policy.'

Many executives have demonstrated that pursuing sustainable development strategies makes good business sense. For example, a 3M manufacturing plant scaled down a wastewater treatment operation by half, simply by running cooling water through its factories repeatedly instead of discharging it after a single use.

Meanwhile Dow's 'Waste Reduction Always Pays' programme, which began in 1986, has fostered more than 700 projects, and saved millions of dollars a year. And in a Westinghouse metal finishing factory in Puerto Rico, the company reduced 'dragout' - the contamination accidentally carried from one tank to another - by 75% simply by shaking the tank to remove solids before releasing the chemical to the next tank.

Pacific Gas and Electric decided that energy conservation was a more profitable investment than nuclear power, and McDonald's made its well-publicized move from plastics to paper the cornerstone of a much broader, but less visible, waste reduction strategy. The managers of these businesses clearly believe that environmentalism has something to offer business.

In an interview with Tomorrow magazine, John Elkington of environmental consultancy SustainAbility says: 'We are seeing the birth of corporate environmentalism. In fact the main impetus for sustainable development in the future will probably come from business.' There are other significant developments too, Elkington points out.

Many consumers are now prepared to pay more for environmentally responsible products. And the emergence of ethical investment funds has thrown the spotlight onto corporate environmental performance. Also significant, says Elkington, is that companies are changing from within, rather than simply responding to external pressure from consumers and environmentalists.

ENHANCING MANAGEMENT SYSTEMS

The concept of sustainable development needs to be incorporated into the policies and processes of a business if it is to follow sustainable development principles. This does not mean that new management methods need to be invented. Rather, it requires a new cultural orientation and extensive refinements to systems, practices and procedures. The two main areas of the management system that must be changed are those concerned with:

- A greater accountability to non-traditional stakeholders;
- Continuous improvement of reporting practices.

Developing an effective management framework for sustainable development requires addressing both decision-making and governance. The concept of sustainable development must be integrated both into business planning and into management information and control systems. Senior management must provide reports that measure performance against these strategies. Governance is increasingly important because of the growing accountability of the corporation and its senior management. Information and reporting systems must support this need. Decision-making at all levels must become more responsive to the issues arising from sustainable development. Seven steps are required for managing an enterprise according to sustainable development principles. These are set out below.

Perform a Stakeholder Analysis

A stakeholder analysis is required in order to identify all the parties that are directly or indirectly affected by the enterprise's operations. It sets out the issues, concerns and information needs of the stakeholders with respect to the organization's sustainable development activities. A company's existence is directly linked to the global environment as well as to the community in which it is based. In carrying out its activities, a company must maintain respect for human dignity, and strive towards a society where the global environment is protected.

At the beginning of this century, company strategies were directed primarily towards earning the maximum return for shareholders and investors.

Businesses were not expected to achieve any other social or environmental objectives. Exploitation of natural and human resources was the norm in many industries, as was a lack of regard for the wellbeing of the communities in which the enterprise operated. In short, corporations were accountable only to their owners.

Today, business enterprises in developed countries operate in a more complicated, and more regulated, environment. Numerous laws and regulations govern their activities, and make their directors accountable to a broader range of stakeholders. Sustainable development extends the stakeholder group even further, by including future generations and natural resources.

Identifying the parties that have a vested interest in a business enterprise is a central component of the sustainable development concept, and leads to greater corporate accountability. Developing a meaningful approach to stakeholder analysis is a vital aspect of this management system, and one of the key differences between sustainable and conventional management practices.

The stakeholder analysis begins by identifying the various groups affected by the business's activities. These include shareholders, creditors, regulators, employees, customers, suppliers, and the community in which the enterprise operates. It must also include people who are affected, or who consider themselves affected, by the enterprise's effect on the biosphere and on social capital.

This is not a case of altruism on the company's part, but rather good business. Companies that understand what their stakeholders want will be able to capitalize on the opportunities presented. They will benefit from a better informed and more active workforce, and better information in the capital markets. In identifying stakeholder groups, management should consider every business activity and operating location. Some stakeholders, such as shareholders, may be common to all activities or locations. Others, such as local communities, will vary according to business location and activity. Finally, the stakeholder analysis needs to consider the effect of the business's activities on the environment, the public at large, and the needs of future generations.

After the stakeholders have been identified, management should prepare a description of the needs and expectations that these groups have. This should set out both current and future needs, in order to capture sustainable development concept. The key is to analyze how the organization's activities affect each set of stakeholders, either positively or negatively.

Developing these statements of needs and expectations requires dialogue with each stakeholder group. To this end, some companies have established community advisory panels. Similar groups made up of employees, shareholders and suppliers have been used to help management better understand their needs and expectations. Because the needs of stakeholder groups are constantly evolving, monitoring them is an ongoing process.

The stakeholder analysis may reveal conflicting expectations. For example, customers may demand new, environmentally safe products, while employees might be concerned that such a policy could threaten their jobs. Shareholders, meanwhile, may be wary about the return on their investment. A stakeholder analysis can be a useful way to identify areas of potential conflict among stakeholder groups before they materialize.

SET SUSTAINABLE DEVELOPMENT POLICIES AND OBJECTIVES

The next objective is to articulate the basic values that the enterprise expects its employees to follow with respect to sustainable development, and to set targets for operating performance. Senior management is responsible for formulating a sustainable development policy for its organization, and for establishing specific objectives. Sustainable development means more than just 'the environment'. It has social elements as well, such as the alleviation of poverty and distributional equity.

It also takes into account economic considerations that may be absent from a strictly 'environmental' viewpoint. In particular, it emphasizes maintaining or enhancing the world's capital endowment, and highlights limits to society's ability to substitute manmade capital for natural capital. Nevertheless, a policy on environmental responsibility is a good first step towards the broader concerns of sustainable development.

Management should incorporate stakeholder expectations into a broad policy statement that sets out the organization's mission with respect to sustainable development. This policy statement would guide the planning process and put forward values towards which management, employees and other groups such as suppliers are expected to strive. Drafting a policy statement that is both inspirational and capable of influencing behaviour is a challenging task. However, the benefits justify the effort.

The following policy statement was developed by the Dow Chemical Company: The operating units of the Dow Chemical Company are committed to continued excellence, leadership and stewardship in protecting and conserving the environment for future generations. This is a primary management responsibility as well as the responsibility of every employee worldwide. We are sensitive to the concerns of the public and accountable to them for our decisions and actions.

We believe in the responsible integration of environmental and economic considerations in all decisions affecting our operations. We are continuously reducing our emissions to protect human health and the environment. Our goal is the elimination of wastes and emissions. Policy statements like this one should be developed and implemented in a way that visibly involves directors and senior management.

A survey by DRT International of European companies found that half of the respondents have board members who are responsible for environmental issues. The report adds: The amount of time spent on environmental issues at board level varies greatly between countries and sectors. The greatest involvement is found in the chemical and pharmaceutical industries and in utilities. These sectors devote significant resources to planning green strategies and establishing sophisticated environmental management systems. The lowest involvement is in tourism and financial services, where none of the companies surveyed had board-level appointments.

There are many benefits in actively involving the board of directors in the development of a sustainable development policy. It is the board of directors that determines overall priorities and sets the tone for management and employees. By itself, the board's commitment will not guarantee that a sustainable development policy will be effectively implemented. However, the absence of that commitment will certainly make it difficult to implement the policy.

While statements of broad policy on sustainable development are important, senior management and directors should supplement their policy statement with a series of specific objectives.

For example, the following statement of policy and objectives, developed by Northern Telecom, illustrates the desirable scope and level of specificity: Recognizing the critical link between a healthy environment and sustained economic growth, we are committed to leading the telecommunications industry in protecting and enhancing the environment.

Such stewardship is indispensable to our continued business success. Therefore, wherever we do business, we will take the initiative in developing innovative solutions to those environmental issues that affect our business. We will:

- Integrate environmental considerations into our business planning and decisionmaking processes, including product research and development, new manufacturing methods and acquisitions/divestitures;
- Identify, assess and manage environmental risks associated with our operations and products throughout their life cycle, to reduce or eliminate the likelihood of adverse consequences;
- Comply with all applicable legal and regulatory requirements and, to the extent we determine it appropriate, adopt more stringent standards for the protection of our employees and the communities in which we operate;
- Establish a formal Environmental Protection Program, and set specific, measurable goals;
- Establish assurance programs, including regular audits, to assess the success of the Environmental Protection Program in meeting regulatory requirements, program goals and good practices;

- To the extent that proven technology **will allow**, eliminate or reduce harmful discharges, hazardous materials and waste;
- Make reduction, reuse and recycling the guiding principles and means by which we achieve our goals;
- Prepare and make public an annual report summarizing our environmental activities;
- Work as advocates with our suppliers, customers and business partners to jointly achieve the highest possible environmental standards;
- Build relationships with other environmental stakeholders - including governments, the scientific community, educational institutions, public interest groups and the general public - to promote the development and communication of innovative solutions to industry environmental problems;
- Provide regular communications to, and training for, employees to heighten awareness of, and pride in, environmental issues.

It is important that sustainable development objectives be clear, concise and, wherever possible, expressed in measurable terms. Establishing measurable objectives is essential if management and others are to be able to assess whether their business activities have met the established objectives.

In setting these objectives, management will need to determine the appropriate level of aggregation. For example, one objective might be to set measurable performance targets for waste reduction at all operating locations. This goal would then be supported by more detailed objectives for each operating location.

After the sustainable development objectives have been established, management should compare its **competitive** and financial strategies against these targets. In some areas, business strategies will be consistent with the sustainable development objectives. In others, existing strategies may be incomplete or in conflict with them. Consequently, strategies may have to be modified.

It is important to ensure that the sustainable development objectives that are established complement the enterprise's existing competitive strategies. In other words, sustainable development should provide an additional dimension to business strategy. It provides senior management with an additional benchmark against which business strategies and performance should be assessed.

An effective external monitoring system is necessary for directors and senior management, in order to ensure that sustainable development policies, objectives and management systems are appropriate for the complex and rapidly changing world in which their business operates. Information should be gathered on key subjects, including:

- New and proposed legislation;
- Industry practices and standards;
- Competitors' strategies;
- Community and special interest group policies and activities;
- Trade union concerns;
- Technical developments, such as new process technologies.

For many enterprises, monitoring and influencing external developments means becoming more actively involved in the public policy process. A commitment to sustainable development involves helping to formulate policies that shape external developments, so that industry-wide sustainable development objectives are achieved. To this end, responsible business enterprises are taking leadership roles in industry associations, working with government and special interest groups to achieve positive results for both the enterprise and the stakeholders.

The monitoring of external developments is particularly complex for companies selling to export markets, and even more so for those with production facilities in several countries. Many multinational corporations subscribe to the International Chamber of Commerce principles on environmental management. These include adherence to international environmental performance standards. However, monitoring all the relevant international developments can be a daunting task.

This external monitoring can be integrated into a firm's strategic management process, or else carried out as a separate exercise. Some corporations have social policy committees whose scope covers sustainable development issues. Others have environmental committees with a narrower focus.

Design and Execute an Implementation Plan

It is important to draw up a plan for the management system changes that are needed in order to achieve sustainable development objectives.

Translating sustainable development policies into operational terms is a major undertaking that will affect the entire organization. It involves changing the corporate culture and employee attitudes, defining responsibilities and accountability, and establishing organizational structures, information reporting systems and operational practices.

These changes are normally so substantial that a three-to-five-year plan with one year milestones will be needed.

Managing this type of organizational change requires leadership from senior management. The board of directors, the chief executive officer and other senior executives must be actively involved in the process. They need to lead by example, and to set the tone for the rest of the organization.

As a starting point, after the board and senior management have established their sustainable development objectives, these should be communicated to the various stakeholder groups. Some organizations have ongoing consultation arrangements with stakeholders which facilitates this process. There is little point in embarking on a programme to meet stakeholders' needs without first consulting stakeholders to ascertain what those needs are.

It is also important to determine any modifications that should be made to the organization's systems and processes in order to ensure that day-to-day activities are performed in a manner that is consistent with these objectives. The enterprise's organizational structure should then be reviewed to determine who should take specific responsibility for the sustainable development objectives. In some cases, environmental management committees have been established; in others, a specific department has been established under the leadership of a senior environmental executive.

Some organizations incorporate statements of environmental responsibility into the job descriptions of managers and staff. Clearly defining accountability is essential to successful implementation. Cultural change and retraining should complement the new goals. Reward systems and incentives reflecting the new corporate values should also be considered. Business planning processes should be modified to reflect the sustainable development priorities, the expanded stakeholder consultation process, and external monitoring needs. Management information systems should be enhanced, in order to ensure that management and employees receive the information they need to assess their performance against the objectives. Marketing activities should consider customers' needs regarding sustainability. This will require changes to the organization's market research efforts. This feedback can affect the way products are designed, produced, packaged, marketed and promoted. In some cases, new markets may be added or existing markets redefined. Meanwhile production processes and operating procedures must be assessed against regulations, industry practices or internal standards, in order to determine areas for improvement. This represents an opportunity for the company to develop innovative production processes.

Regulatory requirements are easily identifiable, although they continually evolve. Sustainable development criteria are less precise, and are generally not yet clearly manifested in regulations. The use of industry practices as performance norms is expanding rapidly, and in some cases these standards exceed regulatory requirements. The chemical industry's 'Responsible Care' programme is one example of industry standards that companies can use to foster improvements in their processes and practices. Another popular tool is benchmarking. At the same time, managers responsible for procurement must reassess their choice of suppliers, in terms of their products and the way in which they are produced, to ensure that the company's sustainable development objectives are fostered through its purchasing activities.

Financial planning should consider the capital requirements for process changes, as well as possible tax incentives and the financial effect of new mechanisms such as credits for waste recovery. A successful implementation plan depends on 'rethinking the corporation' if it is to respond to the paradigm shift associated with sustainable development. It is important to address not only the positive forces for change but also barriers and sources of resistance. While the basic management framework may remain intact, substantial changes will probably be needed in the culture, the organization and its systems. The plan must have full 'buy-in' if it is to be effective. This in turn requires broad consultation and cultural change.

Develop a Supportive Corporate Culture

In order to ensure that the organization and its people give their backing to the sustainable development policies, an appropriate corporate culture is essential. In the process of implementing sustainable development or environmental management policies, many companies have experienced a kind of organizational renewal. The increased participation of employees not only generates practical ideas, but also increases enthusiasm for the programme itself. Most customers and employees enjoy being part of an organization that is committed to operating in a socially responsible manner. Implementing sustainable development objectives will probably require managers to change their attitudes. This may be accomplished only after retraining. For example, some executives may feel that their sole responsibility is to maximize the wealth of the enterprise's owners. As a result, they may have difficulty understanding the sustainable development concept and in accepting it as a legitimate business objective. Meanwhile some managers may not be accustomed to identifying the need for ecoefficient practices such as energy efficiency and recycling. Some may never have explicitly considered the effect of their actions on any stakeholder group other than shareholders. Others may resist changing the way in which their performance is measured.

Managers of multinational corporations may not think it appropriate to redesign their programmes in order to ensure that contribute to sustainable development in poorer countries. Effective communication is essential. Internally, all levels of management, and all employees, must understand the policies and objectives that have been established. For business enterprises, this means broadening the outlook of many people, including some senior executives. Dr Frank Frantisak of Noranda Inc. emphasizes the importance of communication:

The fundamental need in Canadian corporations is the promotion of environmental consciousness throughout the whole organization, from senior management down to the plant floor. Environmental concerns need to be part of everyday communications and decision-making at all levels. Executives need to be regularly asking division managers: Is your operation in compliance? What progress is being made with your action plan? Division managers need to be putting these questions, in turn, to the plant and facility staff.

Employees can have a strong influence on corporate culture and on a company's environmental performance. The DRT International survey of European companies reports that:

Just over half of the companies surveyed invite direct suggestions from employees on environmental issues. About 80% of the companies that invite suggestions have changed their products or processes as a result, while only 54% of all respondents have made such changes. This happens not only in environmentally advanced countries such as Switzerland and Norway, but also in Hungary, where employees are keen to tackle the country's considerable environmental problems. The concept of sustainable development requires organizations to develop a culture that emphasizes employee participation, continuous learning and improvement. The International Chamber of Commerce explains the process of continual improvement thus: ...To continue to improve corporate policies, programmes and environmental performance, taking into account technical developments, scientific understanding, consumer needs and community expectations, with legal regulations as a starting point and to apply the same environmental criteria internationally.

Internal reporting systems can have a significant effect on corporate culture. They must be designed to reinforce positive behaviour with respect to sustainable development. They also need to be linked to the enterprise's recognition and promotion systems, The active and visible involvement of senior executives and directors can be a powerful force in forming attitudes, and in creating a supportive culture in which sustainable business practices can flourish. Executives are the people who set the policies and the norms by which business is done.

Equally, it is important that the board provide an oversight in the allocation of responsibilities for sustainable development objectives. This umbrella role should include ensuring that responsibilities are assigned in a manner that holds key executives accountable. It also means ensuring that reward and promotion systems recognize those people who achieve, or help to achieve, sustainable development objectives.

Develop Measures and Standards of Performance

The implementation of sustainable development objectives, and the preparation of meaningful reports on performance, require appropriate means of measuring performance.

Management control, as well as external reporting, depends in part on the availability of timely information about company operations. This is needed in order to allow management to assess performance against external and internal performance standards, using appropriate performance measures. Information systems will therefore need to be reviewed, to enable the necessary reports to be provided to management. The measures used to assess and report on performance will be influenced by the company's sustainable development objectives, and by standards that have been established by government and other public agencies. For example, performance targets may be set in terms of emission levels and energy usage per tonne of output, or perhaps working hours lost due to accident or illness. The information generated must be in the right units if actual performance is to be compared with the set targets. This might require new measuring procedures to be introduced.

In many cases, companies are ahead of governments in establishing sustainable development performance criteria. However, as society becomes more aware of environmental issues and exerts more pressure for action, government can be expected to take on a more influential role. There is a significant opportunity for the business sector to work with governments in establishing performance measures and standards, and to help develop reporting and monitoring systems that are cost-effective and which meet the needs of both the public and business. While external standards, measures and reporting systems are needed, they take time to develop and implement, especially if consultation is required. Businesses should not wait for such standards to be developed before setting sustainable development objectives and measuring the sustainability of their activities.

PREPARE REPORTS

The next step in the process is to develop meaningful reports for internal management and stakeholders, outlining the enterprise's sustainable development objectives and comparing performance against them. Directors and senior executives use internal reports to measure performance, make decisions and monitor the implementation of their policies and strategies. Shareholders, creditors, employees and customers, as well as the public at large, use external corporate reports to evaluate the performance of a corporation, and to hold the directors and senior executives accountable for achieving financial, social and environmental objectives. Regulators and government officials add to the task by requiring an ever-expanding degree of disclosure, in order to ensure compliance with their regulations. While financial reports continue to be a fundamental component of corporate reporting, they are now only one of many types of report issued annually by a corporation. It is important to narrow the gap between the way economic activity is measured and the way in which the use of natural resources is evaluated. For example, financial statements do not illustrate the degree to which an enterprise invests in pollution control and conserves resources. As a result, companies that do not invest in environmental protection may present financial statements with lower costs and higher earnings than those which do.

The system needs incentives, and reliable information, in order to ensure that there are rewards for positive actions. It is ironic that business activity which destroys habitats and pollutes air, land and water produces 'income' and contributes to gross national product. Decision-makers within businesses and governments need a more relevant reporting system. A system that provides a meaningful picture of a company's sustainability achievements is essential for strengthening accountability. This is necessary if an effective relationship is to be maintained with stakeholder groups.

Internally, several companies now ask their line managers to include in their regular reporting procedures a statement on whether they have achieved the environmental and sustainable development targets. Similarly, the board of directors should receive periodic reports from senior management on whether these objectives have been achieved. External reporting on sustainable development issues can take a number of different formats. Some organizations are experimenting with special reports for particular stakeholder groups, such as employees. Others provide a general-purpose report on environmental activities. Still others include the subject of environmental and social issues in a separate section of their annual reports. Every business enterprise should publish, at least once a year, an external 'sustainable development report'. Ultimately, a universal format for such reports will be desirable. In the meantime, managers and boards of directors should decide on the organization and content of reports.

Enhance Internal Monitoring Processes

On an ongoing basis it will be important to develop mechanisms to help directors and senior managers ensure that the sustainable development policies are being implemented. Performance monitoring is well established as an important element of the management process. In many areas, it is directly linked to reporting. The key to any system's effectiveness is whether the management monitors operations and outputs on an ongoing basis.

Monitoring can take many forms, such as:

- Reviewing reports submitted by middle managers;
- Touring operating sites and observing employees performing their duties;
- Holding regular meetings with subordinates to review reports and to seek input on how the procedures and reporting systems might be improved;
- Implementing an environmental auditing programme.

Organizing internal environmental audits is a practical way to monitor the implementation of management policies. For example, many organizations now perform internal audits to monitor compliance with environmental policies and legislation. These normally require multidisciplinary teams of experts (for example engineers, auditors and scientists) who possess the necessary knowledge and experience, both in auditing and in the areas being audited.

The following definition of environmental auditing was developed in 1989 by the International Chamber of Commerce's working party on environmental auditing: A management tool comprising a systematic, documented, periodic and objective evaluation of how well environmental organization, management and equipment are performing, with the aim of helping to safeguard the environment by:

(i) Facilitating management control of environmental practices;

(ii) Assessing compliance with company policies, which would include meeting regulatory requirements.

In Europe, the Commission of the European Community has adopted guidelines on environmental auditing of industrial activities. Such audits are voluntary but must follow EU guidelines, including the publication of a statement on the audit results by the company, verified by an accredited auditor. The objective is to give companies more control over their environmental performance, and to increase public awareness.

Management Leadership

Establishing sustainable development objectives, systems and monitoring mechanisms requires leadership on the part of senior management, and a commitment to continuous improvement.

The Role of the Board

Without the active involvement of the board of directors, it will be difficult for an organization to implement sustainable business practices. Corporations are encouraged to establish a 'social responsibility committee', responsible for setting corporate policies on sustainable development and for dealing with issues such as health and safety, personnel policies, environmental protection, and codes of business conduct. This list is not all-encompassing.

The committee's exact responsibilities should be dictated by individual business circumstances. Nevertheless, there may be a need to establish a 'minimum' set of responsibilities. It is important that corporate sustainable development policies be implemented consistently throughout an organization. Too many business enterprises observe variable levels of corporate ethics and integrity, depending on the country in which they are operating. This double standard is inconsistent with the concept of sustainable development, and ensuring that it does not prevail is an important role of the directors. The board also has a role in monitoring the implementation of its policies. It should receive regular reports on how the policies are implemented, and should be accountable to its stakeholders on the company's performance against these policies.

Self-assessment

The first step for businesses in adopting sustainable development principles is to assess their current position. Management should know the degree to which the company's activities line up with sustainable development principles. This requires evaluating the company's overall strategy, the performance of specific operations, and the effect of particular activities.

This process should compare the company's current performance with the expectations of the stakeholders. Management philosophies and systems should be reviewed; the scope of public disclosures on sustainability topics should be analyzed; and the ability of current information systems to produce the required data should be evaluated.

Various self-assessment devices are available to help this process, such as the GEMI and CERES questionnaires, as well as material tailored to specific industries – for example, the North American chemical industry's 'Responsible Care' programme.

Deciding on a Strategy

Once managers have gained an understanding of how its own operations shape up, they should gauge the performance of other, comparable organizations. Comparisons against the standards set by other industries and environmental groups can be instructive. This task should be relatively easy if there is reasonable public disclosure, organized industry associations and co-operative sustainable development programmes. However, if these structures do not exist, management could approach other businesses to discuss sharing information and possibly establishing an industry group.

Management should then consider ways to narrow the gap between the current state of the corporation's performance and its objectives for the future. A strategy will need to be developed, outlining where the company hopes to position itself relative to its competitors and its stakeholders' expectations.

A general plan is needed to describe how and when management expects to achieve that goal, together with the various milestones it will reach along the way.

Senior management should review and approve the strategy and the plan before submitting them to the board of directors for final approval. Because of the pervasiveness of sustainable development, it is essential that members of the senior management team (representing all facets of the company's activities) 'buy in' to the project. Anything less than full commitment may doom the plan to failure.

Strategy Implementation

Once the strategy and the general plan have been approved, detailed plans should be prepared indicating how the new strategy will affect operations, management systems, information systems and reporting. These should set out measurable goals to be achieved in each area, and explain how progress will be monitored. They should also specify spending and training requirements. These plans should be developed through consultation with employees throughout the organization, possibly with the assistance of outside specialists. It will be a timeconsuming and dynamic process, which will entail frequent modifications as input is obtained from several sources. Once finalized, the plans should be approved by senior management and, ideally, by the board of directors as well.

Small Business and Private Company Considerations

Applying the proposed framework will be a challenge for all enterprises, but smaller businesses may encounter additional challenges. Besides sustainability reporting, smaller businesses will have to adapt to the new corporate climate with less in-house expertise, fewer resources and less formal management structures than larger corporations. It will be difficult for them to keep abreast of ever-changing regulatory requirements. Fortunately, small businesses can find much of the expertise they require through industry associations, chambers of commerce, corporate environmental groups (such as GEMI in the USA), national and international business-government groups (such as the European Green Table), management consultants and universities.

There is also a growing body of literature, some of which deals with the experiences of companies that have integrated sustainable development into their operations. The limited resources of small businesses can be offset by co-operative ventures with other companies. These may, for example, take the form of committees which monitor developments and serve as a forum for exchanging ideas. To the extent that different companies have similar stakeholders, they can compare notes on their stakeholders' needs and expectations and how they plan to address them. These cooperative ventures could be more complex, and include formal industry programmes dealing with matters such as performance standards, monitoring and technological research.

Once the expertise and resource issues have been addressed, the generally less formal management structures found in small businesses can be a positive advantage. There will be fewer people to educate within the enterprise, and there will usually be less resistance to change. In addition, there are usually no formal committees to whom the new strategies must be 'sold', and no lengthy review and approval procedures to slow the process down. The 'hands on' management style common to smaller businesses can also aid the monitoring function: management will be well positioned to spot problems and to make the necessary adjustments. The road to implementing a sustainable development philosophy will be different for smaller businesses, but with ingenuity, perseverance and cooperation, they can achieve the desired result.

Can you imagine you're ninety years old and still hiking up mountains with your grandchildren, bench pressing more than most twenty year olds, and making millions of dollars?

Recently Jack LaLanne, America's first TV fitness guru, turned ninety. Not only is he still sound of mind, in great shape, he's made millions and is still earning more. How does he do it?

You know it is important to eat your fruits and veggies, exercise regularly, avoid drinking and smoking and get enough sleep to stay healthy. To that list Jack LaLanne would add, set clear goals, exercise with weights twice a week, avoid eating between meals and keep your mind active.

Of course you can't just eat well and skip the exercise or avoid the drinking and smoking and skimp on sleep. Jack LaLanne is still going strong at 90 because he does ALL the things required to stay healthy every day.

Marketing your business requires the same comprehensive, disciplined approach Jack LaLanne uses to stay healthy at 90. To attract new clients and retain existing ones you need to set goals, target a need, get attention, prompt action, grow your network, establish credibility, provide a solution, follow up, demonstrate value and stay in touch. These are the ten essential steps to marketing your business.

Like a staircase, the steps are connected and you need to put them together in the proper sequence and use each of them regularly. A common marketing mistake is to focus on just one or two of the above steps and hope for the best. Joan, who owns a sports facility, called last week about her advertising campaign. It was costing her significant dollars but wasn't translating into new clients. What was the problem?

Advertising can help get attention but to be effective it needs to be focused on clients' needs and prompt them to action. Joan's advertising was focused on her solution, not on prospects' needs resulting in a disappointing response. Once she rewrote her ads to target prospects' needs, her response rates and business revenue increased.

Larry's promotional efforts were working but he wasn't having success translating all the attention he was getting into dollars and cents. Thanks to top search engine positioning and hundreds of links to his web site, thousands of people were visiting his site each day. Yet, on average, only five people per day were contacting him about his services. Larry was doing a great job of getting attention but wasn't prompting his prospects to action.

YOUR MARKETING FITNESS

You can have a steady flow of new prospects and clients each month if you adopt a healthy marketing strategy. Here's how.

1. Set Goals : Regularly review your marketing. Assess what's working and what isn't and set objectives for lead generation, client acquisition and retention.
2. Target a Need : Focus your ads, your elevator speech and your marketing copy on prospects' concerns.
3. Get Attention : Prospects need to know that you exist before they will contact you.
4. Prompt Action : In order to get prospects to give you their contact information, inquire about your services or buy your products, prompt them to action. Use your marketing copy and your offers to get prospects to call you, visit your web site or your store, and buy your products and services.
5. Grow Your Network : The more qualified leads you have, the better.
6. Establish Credibility : You need to demonstrate your competence and convince prospects to trust you before they'll make a purchase.
7. Follow Up : Old leads are cold leads. Follow up when leads are fresh. When people contact you, send an immediate email response and give them a call within 24 hours.
8. Provide a Solution : Make sure your products and services are the solution to your prospects' problems.

9. Demonstrate Value : If you want someone to buy, they need to understand the benefits.
10. Stay in Touch : Don't let prospects forget you when they need you and are ready to buy.

If you increased the time you spent working out each day and improved your diet, you'd start to see a difference in a couple of weeks. You'd be stronger and healthier.

Marketing is the same. You need to do all the right things consistently. Start using these ten marketing steps and in a couple of weeks you'll start to see a change. You'll find more prospects contacting you and a steady increase in revenue.

Whether you want to be fit and profitable at 90 or not you can learn from Jack LaLanne's continued health and prosperity. It just takes some discipline and knowledge. Apply both to keep yourself and your business in good health.

ORGANIZATIONAL CULTURE

Organizational culture, or corporate culture, comprises the attitudes, experiences, beliefs and values of an organization. It has been defined as "the specific collection of values and norms that are shared by people and groups in an organization and that control the way they interact with each other and with stakeholders outside the organization. Organizational values are beliefs and ideas about what kinds of goals members of an organization should pursue and ideas about the appropriate kinds or standards of behavior organizational members should use to achieve these goals. From organizational values develop organizational norms, guidelines or expectations that prescribe appropriate kinds of behavior by employees in particular situations and control the behavior of organizational members towards one another"Senior management may try to determine a corporate culture. They may wish to impose corporate values and standards of behavior that specifically reflect the objectives of the organization. In addition, there will also be an extant internal culture within the workforce.

Work-groups within the organization have their own behavioral quirks and interactions which, to an extent, affect the whole system. Task culture can be imported. For example, computer technicians will have expertise, language and behaviors gained independently of the organization, but their presence can influence the culture of the organization as a whole.

Strong/weak Cultures

Strong culture is said to exist where staff respond to stimulus because of their alignment to organizational values.

Conversely, there is weak culture where there is little alignment with organizational values and control must be exercised through extensive procedures and bureaucracy.

Where culture is strong—people do things because they believe it is the right thing to do—there is a risk of another phenomenon, Groupthink. "Groupthink" was described by Irving L. Janis. He defined it as "...a quick and easy way to refer to a mode of thinking that people engage when they are deeply involved in a cohesive ingroup, when members' strivings for unanimity override their motivation to realistically appraise alternatives of action."

This is a state where people, even if they have different ideas, do not challenge organizational thinking, and therefore there is a reduced capacity for innovative thoughts. This could occur, for example, where there is heavy reliance on a central charismatic figure in the organization, or where there is an evangelical belief in the organization's values, or also in groups where a friendly climate is at the base of their identity (avoidance of conflict). In fact groupthink is very common, it happens all the time, in almost every group. Members that are defiant are often turned down or seen as a negative influence by the rest of the group, because they bring conflict.

Innovative organizations need individuals who are prepared to challenge the status quo—be it groupthink or bureaucracy, and also need procedures to implement new ideas effectively.

Classification Schemes

Several methods have been used to classify organizational culture. Some are described below:

Geert Hofstede

Geert Hofstede demonstrated that there are national and regional cultural groupings that affect the behavior of organizations. Hofstede identified five dimensions of culture in his study of national influences:

- *Power distance* - The degree to which a society expects there to be differences in the levels of power. A high score suggests that there is an expectation that some individuals wield larger amounts of power than others. A low score reflects the view that all people should have equal rights.
- *Uncertainty avoidance* reflects the extent to which a society accepts uncertainty and risk.
- *individualism vs. collectivism* - individualism is contrasted with collectivism, and refers to the extent to which people are expected to stand up for themselves, or alternatively act predominantly as a member of the group or organization. However, recent researches have shown that high individualism may not necessarily mean low collectivism, and vice versa.

Research indicates that the two concepts are actually unrelated. Some people and cultures might have both high individualism and high collectivism, for example. Someone who highly values duty to his or her group does not necessarily give a low priority to personal freedom and self-sufficiency

- *Mascúlinity vs. femininity* - refers to the value placed on traditionally male or female values. Male values for example include competitiveness, assertiveness, ambition, and the accumulation of wealth and material possessions.
- *Long vs. short term orientation* - describes a society's "time horizon," or the importance attached to the future versus the past and present. In long term oriented societies, thrift and perseverance are valued more; in short term oriented societies, respect for tradition and reciprocation of gifts and favors are valued more. Eastern nations tend to score especially high here, with Western nations scoring low and the less developed nations very low; China scored highest and Pakistan lowest.

Deal and Kennedy

Deal and Kennedy defined organizational culture as *the way things get done around here*. They measured organizations in respect of:

- Feedback - quick feedback means an instant response. This could be in monetary terms, but could also be seen in other ways, such as the impact of a great save in a soccer match.
- Risk - represents the degree of uncertainty in the organization's activities.

Using these parameters, they were able to suggest four classifications of organizational culture:

- The Tough-Guy Macho Culture. Feedback is quick and the rewards are high. This often applies to fast moving financial activities such as brokerage, but could also apply to a police force, or athletes competing in team sports. This can be a very stressful culture in which to operate.
- The Work Hard/Play Hard Culture is characterized by few risks being taken, all with rapid feedback. This is typical in large organizations, which strive for high quality customer service. It is often characterized by team meetings, jargon and buzzwords.
- The Bet your Company Culture, where big stakes decisions are taken, but it may be years before the results are known. Typically, these might involve development or exploration projects, which take years to come to fruition, such as oil prospecting or military aviation.
- The Process Culture occurs in organizations where there is little or no feedback. People become bogged down with how things are done not with what is to be achieved. This is often associated with bureaucracies. While it is easy to criticize these cultures for being overly cautious or bogged down in red tape, they do produce consistent results, which is ideal in, for example, public services.

Charles Handy

Charles Handy (1985) popularized a method of looking at culture which some scholars have used to link organizational structure to Organizational Culture. He describes:

- a Power Culture which concentrates power among a few. Control radiates from the center like a web. Power Cultures have few rules and little bureaucracy; swift decisions can ensue.

- In a Role Culture, people have clearly delegated authorities within a highly defined structure. Typically, these organizations form hierarchical bureaucracies. Power derives from a person's position and little scope exists for expert power.
- By contrast, in a Task Culture, teams are formed to solve particular problems. Power derives from expertise as long as a team requires expertise. These cultures often feature the multiple reporting lines of a matrix structure.
- A Person Culture exists where all individuals believe themselves superior to the organization. Survival can become difficult for such organizations, since the concept of an organization suggests that a group of like-minded individuals pursue the organizational goals. Some professional partnerships can operate as person cultures, because each partner brings a particular expertise and clientele to the firm.

Edgar Schein

Edgar Schein, an MIT Sloan School of Management professor, defines organizational culture as "the residue of success" within an organization. According to Schein, culture is the most difficult organizational attribute to change, outlasting organizational products, services, founders and leadership and all other physical attributes of the organization. His organizational model illuminates culture from the standpoint of the observer, described by three cognitive levels of organizational culture.

At the first and most cursory level of Schein's model is organizational attributes that can be seen, felt and heard by the uninitiated observer. Included are the facilities, offices, furnishings, visible awards and recognition, the way that its members dress, and how each person visibly interacts with each other and with organizational outsiders.

The next level deals with the professed culture of an organization's members. At this level, company slogans, mission statements and other operational creeds are often expressed, and local and personal values are widely expressed within the organization. Organizational behavior at this level usually can be studied by interviewing the organization's membership and using questionnaires to gather attitudes about organizational membership.

At the third and deepest level, the organization's tacit assumptions are found. These are the elements of culture that are unseen and not cognitively identified in everyday interactions between organizational members. Additionally, these are the elements of culture which are often taboo to discuss inside the organization. Many of these 'unspoken rules' exist without the conscious knowledge of the membership. Those with sufficient experience to understand this deepest level of organizational culture usually become acclimatized to its attributes over time, thus reinforcing the invisibility of their existence. Surveys and casual interviews with organizational members cannot draw out these attributes—rather much more in-depth means is required to first identify then understand organizational culture at this level. Notably, culture at this level is the underlying and driving element often missed by organizational behaviorists.

Using Schein's model, understanding paradoxical organizational behaviors becomes more apparent. For instance, an organization can profess highly aesthetic and moral standards at the second level of Schein's model while simultaneously displaying curiously opposing behavior at the third and deepest level of culture. Superficially, organizational rewards can imply one organizational norm but at the deepest level imply something completely different. This insight offers an understanding of the difficulty that organizational newcomers have in assimilating organizational culture and why it takes time to become acclimatized. It also explains why organizational change agents usually fail to achieve their goals: underlying tacit cultural norms are generally not understood before would-be change agents begin their actions. Merely understanding culture at the deepest level may be insufficient to institute cultural change because the dynamics of interpersonal relationships (often under threatening conditions) are added to the dynamics of organizational culture while attempts are made to institute desired change.

Elements

G. Johnson described a cultural web, identifying a number of elements that can be used to describe or influence Organizational Culture:

- The Paradigm: What the organization is about; what it does; its mission; its values.
- Control Systems: The processes in place to monitor what is going on. Role cultures would have vast rulebooks. There would be more reliance on individualism in a power culture.
- Organizational Structures: Reporting lines, hierarchies, and the way that work flows through the business.
- Power Structures: Who makes the decisions, how widely spread is power, and on what is power based?
- Symbols: These include organizational logos and designs, but also extend to symbols of power such as parking spaces and executive washrooms.
- Rituals and Routines: Management meetings, board reports and so on may become more habitual than necessary.
- Stories and Myths: build up about people and events, and convey a message about what is valued within the organization.

These elements may overlap. Power structures may depend on control systems, which may exploit the very rituals that generate stories which may not be true.

ORGANIZATIONAL CULTURE AND CHANGE

Burman and Evans (2008) argue that it is 'leadership' that affects culture rather than 'management', and describe the difference. When one wants to change an aspect of the culture of an organization one has to keep in consideration that this is a long term project. Corporate culture is something that is very hard to change and employees need time to get used to the new way of organizing. For companies with a very strong and specific culture it will be even harder to change.

Cummings & Worley (2005, p. 491 – 492) give the following six guidelines for cultural change, these changes are in line with the eight distinct stages mentioned by Kotter (1995, p. 2)3:

1. Formulate a clear strategic vision (stage 1,2 & 3 of Kotter, 1995, p. 2)

   In order to make a cultural change effective a clear vision of the firm's new strategy, shared values and behaviours is needed. This vision provides the intention and direction for the culture change (Cummings & Worley, 2005, p.490).

2. Display Top-management commitment (stage 4 of Kotter, 1995, p. 2)

   It is very important to keep in mind that culture change must be managed from the top of the organization, as willingness to change of the senior management is an important indicator (Cummings & Worley, 2005, page 490). The top of the organization should be very much in favour of the change in order to actually implement the change in the rest of the organization. De Caluwé & Vermaak (2004, p 9) provide a framework with five different ways of thinking about change.

3. Model culture change at the highest level (stage 5 of Kotter, 1995, p. 2)

   In order to show that the management team is in favour of the change, the change has to be notable at first at this level. The behaviour of the management needs to symbolize the kinds of values and behaviours that should be realized in the rest of the company. It is important that the management shows the strengths of the current culture as well, it must be made clear that the current organizational does not need radical changes, but just a few adjustments. (See for more: (Deal & Kennedy, 1982; Sathe, 1983; Schall; 1983; Weick, 1985; DiTomaso, 1987)

4. Modify the organization to support organizational change

   The fourth step is to modify the organization to support organizational change.

5. Select and socialize newcomers and terminate deviants (stage 7 & 8 of Kotter, 1995, p. 2)

   A way to implement a culture is to connect it to organizational membership, people can be selected and terminate in terms of their fit with the new culture (Cummings & Worley, 2005, p. 491).

6. Develop ethical and legal sensitivity

   Changes in culture can lead to tensions between organizational and individual interests, which can result in ethical and legal problems for practitioners. This is particularly relevant for changes in employee integrity, control, equitable treatment and job security (Cummings & Worley, 2005, p. 491).

ENTREPRENEURIAL CULTURE

Stephen McGuire defined and validated a model of organizational culture that predicts revenue from new sources. An Entrepreneurial Organizational Culture (EOC) is a system of shared values, beliefs and norms of members of an organization, including valuing creativity and tolerance of creative people, believing that innovating and seizing market opportunities are appropriate behaviors to deal with problems of survival and prosperity, environmental uncertainty, and competitors' threats, and expecting organizational members to behave accordingly.

Critical Views

Writers from Critical management studies have tended to express skepticism about the functionalist and unitarist views of culture put forward by mainstream management thinkers. Whilst not necessarily denying that organizatic ıs are cultural phenomena, they would stress the ways in which cultural assumptions can stifle dissent and reproduce management propaganda and ideology. After all, it would be naive to believe that a single culture exists in all organizations, or that cultural engineering will reflect the interests of all stakeholders within an organization.

In any case, Parker has suggested that many of the assumptions of those putting forward theories of organizational culture are not new. They reflect a long-standing tension between cultural and structural (or informal and formal) versions of what organizations are. Further, it is perfectly reasonable to suggest that complex organizations might have many cultures, and that such sub-cultures might overlap and contradict each other. The neat typologies of cultural forms found in textbooks rarely acknowledge such complexities, or the various economic contradictions that exist in capitalist organizations.

One of the strongest and widely recognised criticisms of theories that attempt to categorise or 'pigeonhole' organisational culture is that put forward by Linda Smircich. She uses the metaphor of a plant root to represent culture, describing that it drives organisations rather than vice versa. Organisations are the product of organisational culture, we are unaware of how it shapes behaviour and interaction (also recognised through Scheins (2002) underlying assumptions) and so how can we categorise it and define what it is?

Measurement

Despite the evidence suggesting their potential usefulness, organisational climate metrics have not been fully exploited as leading safety, health and environmental performance indicators and as an aid to relative risk ranking. Dodsworth et al. are the first researchers to have successfully used PLS modelling techniques to correlate organizational climate metrics with an organisation's safety performance. Further information regarding this research can be obtained from the following link Dodsworth's Homepage

In the context of effectiveness, the repertory grid interview can be used to capture a representation of an organisation's culture or corporate culture - the organisation's construct system. The repertory grid interview process provides a structured way of comparing effective and less effective performance and capturing it in the interviewee's words without imposing someone else's model or way of thinking.

5

ORGANIZATIONAL CLIMATE METRICS

Employing over 58,000 people worldwide, AstraZeneca is a leading pharmaceutical company with sales in over 100 countries, manufacturing in twenty, and major research centres in five. AstraZeneca was formed on 6 April 1999 through the merger of Astra AB of Sweden and Zeneca Group PLC of the UK – two companies with similar science-based cultures and a shared vision of the pharmaceutical industry.

Sales in 2002 totalled \$17.8 billion, with an operating profit of \$4.4 billion . Societal expectations relating to corporate responsibility are higher than ever before. Maintaining society's trust and confidence is an increasing challenge for companies everywhere. Shareholders are of course still looking for a good return on their investment, but they increasingly want assurance that they are investing in a business that delivers shareholder value in a responsible way.

Customers expect high ethical standards as well as high quality products. Local communities only welcome those businesses that can demonstrate good corporate citizenship. Effective corporate responsibility performance depends on achieving an acceptable balance between the economic, environmental and social priorities of sustainable development. Quoting AstraZeneca Chief Executive Sir Tom McKillop :

"Corporate Responsibility is not an add on extra - it is an integral part of all that we do and I am determined that we will continue to be a company that is welcomed as a valued member of the global community".

Safety, health and environmental (SHE) performance is key to building and maintaining effective corporate responsibility. As regulatory frameworks become ever tighter and the cost of business interruptions soars, there is an increasing need for continuous improvement in SHE compliance based on a creative and self-fulfilling compliance culture. The pharmaceutical and other related process industries are characterised by inherently hazardous processes and activities. Besides the obvious areas of safety, health and the environment, organisational decisions and assessments based upon relative risk are made frequently and include:

- The amount of liability and asset insurance to purchase.
- The most appropriate location for new investments, such as new plant or expansion of old.
- To prioritise auditing resource effort.

Identification of business interruption risks.

The challenge for most organisations is how to identify where the greatest SHE risks lie. A number of risk profile identification strategies have been used by industry, including:

Examination of lagging SHE performance indicators such as accident and environmental incident rates.

Examination of leading SHE performance indicators such as the number of 'near miss' or learning event opportunities.

The findings and recommendations of on-site inspections and audits.

Inherent hazard potential of an asset or operation.

Intuition or personal and, or collective 'gut feel'.

A combination of two or more of the above.

Despite the desire to improve SHE performance, accident and incident rates for many commercial and industrial organisations have plateaued. The reason behind the plateau is perhaps that organisations have historically looked toward hardware and procedural control to better improve SHE performance and compliance. Saari suggested that after a certain point, technology alone cannot achieve further improvements in safety. Instead, organisational and cultural factors become more important. Awareness regarding the importance of organisational culture and its relationship to positive SHE performance is growing.

More and more organisations are realising that hardware and procedural improvements do not, by themselves, give rise to tolerable levels of compliance . Assessments have been made that attribute over 50% of industrial-based accidents to factors such as poor management, poor training and other psychological factors. Other studies within the chemical industry have shown that more accidents are attributable to human issues and managerial deficiencies than to weaknesses in technical components. For instance, Powell and Canter, Reason and Layfield highlighted that recognising the contribution of humans to failure of systems has long been an integral part of good engineering design.

Engineers' attempts to quantify the frequency of human failures are generally based upon historical data and are limited to low order human tasks such as, for example, 'wrong button pressed', 'material added in wrong order' and 'processing step missed out'. These foreseeable deviations from routine operating conditions are often identified using processes such as hazard and operability studies (HAZOP). Higher order management failures such as 'inappropriate purchasing strategies' and 'deliberate actions' are often excluded from these studies.

Authors such as Heinrich et al and Porter and Corlett consider that more than 90% of accidents are caused by human factors rather than equipment failures. Powell and Canter found that within the chemical industry, more accidents are attributable to deficiencies in human and management components than to unforeseeable weaknesses in technical components.

The findings of major accident investigations are showing that human cultural factors play an important role in accident causation, prevention and mitigation. Companies are realising that 'rule based' organisational cultures do not adequately ensure satisfactory performance. Two major reasons are identified: firstly, no one carries a rulebook around with them.

Secondly, it is not possible to write rules that encompass all activities and circumstances. Recognising that personnel in all jobs have, to an extent, degrees of interpretive flexibility, the goal of industry should be to ensure that personnel have internalised, via training, their perceptions and the messages that they have received about behaviour that is or is not acceptable. The challenge for highly regulated industries is to find the balance between rule setting and allowing sufficient flexibility to enable personnel to work effectively and efficiently.

There are several possible explanations why industry has generally failed to address human factor issues. The most likely explanation is perhaps that hardware plant and equipment is more tangible (therefore easier to address) than 'human' and 'cultural' factors. Another reason for the failure may be due to a requirement for organisations to reach a level of engineering and procedural maturity before it becomes realistic for them to tackle human factor issues.

The importance of addressing cultural aspects has been highlighted by recent well publicised major loss events such as Chernobyl , Piper Alpha and the Kings Cross fire. Following the 1988 Kings Cross Fire, Judge Fennell wrote:

> *"... a cultural change in management is required throughout the organisation".*

Similarly during the Piper Alpha Inquiry Lord Cullen wrote:

> *" ... it is essential to create a corporate atmosphere or culture in which safety is understood to be and is accepted as, the number one priority".*

More recently, Lord Cullen's inquiry into the 1999 Ladbroke Grove rail accident paid much attention to the role of safety management and culture within the rail industry. The inquiry pointed to evidence that suggests that a large proportion of accidents, incidents and near miss occurrences follow from unsafe acts that are a result of underlying deficiencies in safety management. Thus, the inquiry emphasised the link between 'good safety' and 'good business'. Cullen recognised that a successful safety culture depends on leadership.

The inquiry heard that the fragmentation of the rail industry made it difficult to achieve clear safety leadership within the UK rail industry. Cullen stressed the need for the safety commitment of senior management that should be clearly visible to front line workers and, the need for effective communication of safety goals and objectives along with regular meetings devoted to safety issues. Dyer, Greenstreet Berman Ltd. and the HSE have summarized those good practices that support a positive SHE culture.

The recognition that there is a relationship between organisational culture and safety performance has spawned an increased interest in identification of methods that allow measurement of organisational culture. Organisational culture can be measured and evaluated through organisational climate surveys. Organisational climate surveys can be viewed as surface indicators of an organisation's underlying culture. Culture is a multi-dimensional construct. No one dimension, factor or attribute can therefore adequately describe it. Safety culture is only one of the many dimensions of an organisation's multi-dimensional culture.

A significant amount of research associated with organisational climate surveys exists. These surveys tend to be almost entirely focused toward issues that can be directly associated with safety. The surveys are generally composed of a set of questions that typically require a 'tick box' preference response from 'strongly agree' through 'neutral' to 'strongly disagree'. Researchers typically group survey questions together under hypothesised factors. The response data are often subjected to structural equation modelling techniques to identify the complex relationships between each of the hypothesised factors.

Surveying a number of cultural surveys available in the literature indicated that the number of principal component factors of organisational culture identified ranged from two to nineteen. In addition to variation of the number of factor components, the literature survey indicated that the components themselves varied from survey to survey. Flin et al carried out a thematic survey of eighteen cultural surveys and concluded that all of the themes could be distilled into the following five factors:

- Management/Supervision.
- Safety System.
- Risk.
- Work Pressure.
- Competence.

Unsurprisingly, as is the case with many social science issues, no agreement currently exists as to how many factors or indeed which factors are required to adequately describe organisational culture. Several studies have examined the results of attitudinal surveys and have proposed architectures or underlying structures of the shared perceptions and attitudes toward safety. The models often suggest strengths of relationships and interdependencies of the measured cultural factors.

Although much work has been done regarding the identification and modelling of safety culture factors, significantly less research has been performed in correlating theoretical cultural constructs with broader outcome metrics such as lagging safety performance indicators. A study by HSE found statistically significant relationships between cultural factors and lagging safety indicators such as self-reported injuries and dangerous occurrences.

Coyle et al found a relationship between safety climate factor scores and lost time accident rates, although this relationship was not statistically quantified. Hofman and Stetzer found that safety metrics were related to accident rates. These studies are similar to the majority reviewed in that they focus upon those organisational aspects that are directly related to safety. Little research was found that has examined how other non-safety related organisational factors may affect SHE performance.

In response to these findings, AstraZeneca has started to take a more holistic approach to SHE management in which all the contributing factors to potentially unsafe incidents are considered.

This holistic approach requires examination and development of a range of issues including the traditional safety technology and engineering controls together with management systems and human factor issues.

AstraZeneca recognises that employees' attitudes and satisfactions can strongly influence its ability to meet business objectives. In an attempt to measure employee attitudes and behaviours the company has administered three 'Focus' surveys. The first survey was conducted in 2000, the second in 2002, the third in 2004. All AstraZeneca sites took part in each of the surveys. About 42,000 personnel responded to the 2002 survey, making it 5 times larger than the next largest comparable survey found in the literature review. The Focus surveys were used to measure employees' attitudes and satisfactions in ten factor areas. Comparison of the Focus 2002 survey questions with established organisational culture research indicated that the Focus data set would be a useful and effective measurement tool that would allow AstraZeneca to measure its organisational culture.

It is imperative that any safety performance indicators used to correlate with organisational climate metrics are comparable and robust. A sufficient number of sites must have comparable, if not identical, metrics for the correlational exercise to be valid. The lack of a consistent set of organisational climate and performance metrics across industry is probably the principal reason for the lack of research in this area. Despite their potential usefulness, organisational climate metrics have not yet been exploited by industry as a proactive measure of SHE performance or as an aid to relative risk ranking.

As part of AstraZeneca corporate procedures, each site within the company is required to report its SHE performance on a quarterly basis. Guidance is given within the corporate reporting procedure to ensure consistent reporting.

The availability of the Focus 2002 survey and SHE performance indicators covering several countries, presents a unique opportunity to explore the links between organisational culture and SHE performance. The research objectives listed in Table 1 were formulated to address this opportunity.

Question Number	Research Questions
1	What is the current understanding of organisational culture and its relationship to lagging SHE performance indicators?
2	What statistical techniques have been used in previous research to measure organisational culture?
3	What statistical techniques have been used to link organisational culture with lagging SHE performance indicators?
4	What statistical techniques are most appropriate to determine the relationship between organisational culture and lagging SHE performance indicators?
5	Based upon organisational culture metrics, what statistical techniques are most appropriate to discriminate between nations and sites of different SHE performance?
6	Does the AstraZeneca Focus 2002 survey have the ability to measure AstraZeneca's organisational culture?
7	Does AstraZeneca have sufficient information to allow investigation of its organisational culture and its relationship to lagging SHE indicators?
8*	Can metrics of organisational culture be used to predict site SHE performance?
9*	Can metrics of organisational culture, not directly related to SHE, be used to predict unit/site SHE performance?

10* Does the simultaneous measurement of several organisational culture metrics improve the researcher's ability to better predict site SHE performance compared to the use of a single measure of organisational culture?

11* Can a single model of organisational culture be used to predict SHE performance in more than one nation?

12* How many organisational culture latent constructs are correlated with lagging SHE performance indicators?

13* Does the measurement of organisational climate metrics offer a robust tool for industry to predict SHE performance and perform relative risk ranking?

14* Can the responses to an organisational culture survey be used to classify nations?

15* What organisational culture questions can be used to classify nations?

16* Can the responses to an organisational culture survey be used to classify sites based upon SIFR performance?

17* What organisational culture questions can be used to discriminate between those sites with good safety performance and those with poor safety performance?

Table 1.1 (continued) Research questions

* Answers to these research questions will contribute to existing knowledge.

Answering the above questions will enable industry to determine the usefulness of organisational culture metrics to predict SHE performance and allow identification of those organisational culture factors that most influence it.

This chapter explores the current understanding of organisational culture and its relationship to SHE performance. Specifically, the review examines:

- The definitions of organisational culture.
- How organisational culture is measured.
- The established relationships between organisational culture and lagging SHE performance indicators.
- The statistical techniques that are appropriate to establish the structure of organisational culture and the relationship between it and lagging SHE performance indicators.
- The requirements of robust lagging SHE performance indicators.

HUMAN NATURE, CULTURE AND BEHAVIORS

All humans are individuals and as such, given a set of circumstances, think, feel and react in different ways that have evolved throughout their lifetime. Once a particular pattern of thinking and feeling has been established the person must unlearn it before learning something that replaces it. As most adults have experienced, the process of unlearning and relearning is more difficult than learning something new. Hofstede compares human thoughts, feelings and reactions to the way in which a computer program works, calling them the 'software of the mind'. The mental programming within individuals starts during infancy and is influenced by the environment in which a person is brought up. Culture is learned, not inherited. Culture is specific to a group; it is not an individual construct. Human nature differs from culture in that the former is inherited from parents and is not learned. Examples of human nature include: The way in which humans observe their environment and talk about it. The ability to laugh, cry, make love, express emotions and to be angry.

Hofstede compares human nature to the 'operating system of a computer'.

A person's human nature is not directly observable by others. Human nature such as feelings and emotions are influenced and modified by culture. Human nature is shared by all other humans. Personality differs from culture and nature in that human personality is specific to an individual. Personality is partly learned and partly inherited.

Culture Symbols - Symbols are the most visible and superficial part of a culture that can be seen by others of the same and differing cultures.

Symbols are those objects, words and gestures that mean something and are recognised by those sharing the same culture.

Examples of symbols include jargon, hairstyles, Coca-Cola, religious and status symbols. With time old symbols may give way to newer more fashionable symbols. Being superficial they are easily copied by individuals belonging to other cultures.

Culture Heroes - Culture heroes are those persons, dead, alive, real or imaginary that exhibit characteristics that are well respected within that culture. Heroes range from presidents to comic book characters.

Culture Rituals - Rituals are those practices that are exercised by members of a culture that are considered socially essential.

Examples of rituals include handshaking when meeting someone, religious ceremonies and the way in which business and other meetings are conducted.

Culture Values - Unlike culture symbols, culture values are not visible to an observer. Hofstede describes values as a 'feeling with an arrow attached to it' such as:

Evil	←	Versus	→	Good
Dirty	←	Versus	→	Clean
Ugly	←	Versus	→	Beautiful
Unnatural	←	Versus	→	Natural
Abnormal	←	Versus	→	Normal
Paradoxical	←	Versus	→	Logical
Irrational	←	Versus	→	Rational

It is widely accepted by developmental psychologists that a person's values are well established by the age of ten, after which it becomes difficult for a person to change them. Several researchers have studied the effect of the environment surrounding an individual. Davies and Powell wrote: "People are neither deterministically controlled by their environments nor entirely self-determining. Instead they exist in a state of reciprocal determinism whereby they and their environments influence one another in a perpetual dynamic interplay".

Bandura explains psychosocial functioning in terms of a triadic reciprocal causation whereby an individual's internal psychological factors, the environment which they are in and the behaviour they exhibit, all operate as interacting determinants that influence one another bi-directionally.

Bandura's model recognises that culture is affected by the relative strength of the three factors. It also takes into account that the culture is dynamic in nature. Cooper has built upon Bandura's reciprocal model stating that it is an ideal framework by which to analyse safety culture.

Cooper proposed that it is an ideal framework as it recognises those psychological, behavioural and situational elements which are found in a number of researchers' accident causation models. In his paper Cooper suggests that, because Bandura's model is composed of three elements, it allows 'triangulation' and multi-level analysis. Cooper suggests that Bandura's:

- 'Situation' element may be measured by an objective audit of the safety management system.
- 'Behavioural' element may be measured by sampling and measurement of behavioural indicators.
- 'Person' element may be measured by a perceptual audit of the safety climate.

Measurement of these three elements allows a more holistic measurement of safety culture. No research furthering Cooper's triangulation hypothesis was found during the literature review.

ORGANISATIONAL AND NATIONAL CULTURES

Culture is found at national, regional, and organisational levels. The way in which organisations' attitudes are expressed may be described as 'corporate (or organisational) culture'.

The way corporate culture is perceived may be described as 'corporate (or organisational) climate'. Other definitions of corporate culture and climate exist and are outlined below. Both corporate culture and corporate climate contain elements of safety culture and safety climate.

Within any organisational culture, many layers of sub-cultures may exist, ranging through county, site, function, and department to individual work teams. Schein summarises culture as: "The way in which a group of people solves problems and reconciles dilemmas".

Ostrom et al define culture as: " .... norms or patterns of perceptions, speech and even building design features that make the culture what it is". Citing Rentch, Zohar's definition of organisational culture refers to shared perceptions among members of an organisation with regard to organisational policies, procedures and practices. Zohar then goes on to suggest a multilevel interpretation; top level managers are concerned with policy making and the establishment of procedures to facilitate policy implementation whereas, at the lower hierarchical levels, supervisors execute the policies by making and establishing procedures. In Zohar's model there are therefore two distinct levels of organisational culture.

James and Jones distinguished metrics of organisational climate that are based on the structural properties of organisations (such as size, leadership, systems and organisational structure) from perceptions held by employees about aspects of their organisational environment. Trompenaars and Hampden-Turner propose that national cultural differences are manifested under three headings, namely, relationships with people, attitudes towards time, and the environment in which the culture exists.

Inkeles and Levinson performed an extensive survey of English-language literature associated with national cultures and suggested that the following issues are common to the functioning of societies and of individuals within them:

- Relation to authority.
- Conception of self, in particular;
    - o the relationship between individual and society, and
    - o the individual's concept of masculinity and femininity.
- Ways of dealing with conflicts including the control of aggression and the expression of feelings.

Hofstede studied the data from a survey conducted by IBM. The survey questioned the values of IBM employees in fifty countries throughout the world. After statistically analysing the results of the survey Hofstede concluded that different national cultures can be distinguished by the following four factors:

1) Social inequality, including relationship with authority.
2) The relationship between the individual and the group.
3) Concepts of masculinity and femininity i.e. the social implications of having been born a boy or a girl.
4) Ways of dealing with uncertainty, relating to the control of aggression and the expression of emotions.

It is noted that Hofstede's conclusions above are very similar to the earlier work performed by Inkeles and Levinson [91] summarised above.

It has been argued that it is inappropriate to attempt to separate SHE culture from general business management culture. Indeed, Apostolakis and Wu suggested that:

"When the subject is culture, we must question the wisdom of separating safety culture from the culture that exists with respect to normal plant operation and power production. The dependencies between them are much stronger because they are due to common work processes and organisational factors".

Ball and Scotney suggest a "composite" holistic view of culture as being the product of organisational and personal factors.

This observation is consistent with the organisational sub-cultures phenomenon described below. If such an holistic culture does exist it may be possible to measure one aspect of business culture and extrapolate the results to SHE culture.

It is important to recognise that groups of individuals within an organisation do not have the same set of values, beliefs, behaviours etc. These differences give rise to sub-cultures. Neal et al found a relationship between organisational safety climate and safety behaviours. Mearns et al found evidence of sub-cultures during a survey of ten off-shore installations. These sub-cultures were classified under the headings of age, prior accident involvement, job grade, shift pattern and occupation. McDonald et al identified sub-cultures that were able to discriminate between technicians and management personnel within aircraft maintenance organisations. Any metric of organisational culture therefore needs to take into account the distribution of culture within the organisation.

Trompenaars and Hampden-Turner suggest that the way in which different cultures perceive one another is dependent upon the differences in the mean and normal distribution of culture. In certain situations the cultural overlap between two groups may be such that many of the individuals within the two groups may share common cultural elements. Stereotyping occurs when one group focuses on cultural elements of another cultural group that are not common to its own. According to Cooper the concept of 'safety culture' was first mentioned in the 1987 report on the 1986 Chernobyl disaster. Cooper proposed that safety culture should be the dominant sub-component of an organisation's culture when the organisation is operating within a high-risk industry sector. Cooper also recognised that the prevalent trend of organisational downsizing and restructuring will exert a considerable influence on organisational safety culture development and visa versa. A review of the literature indicates that there are many definitions of safety culture and safety climate. Although the definitions of culture and climate are similar, they do differ in important respects. Safety culture has been defined as:

"the embodiment of a set of principles which loosely define what an organisation is like in terms of health and safety".

" .... the product of individual and group values, attitudes, competencies, and patterns of behaviour that determine the commitment to, and the style and proficiency of, an organisation's health and safety programmes. Organisations with a positive safety culture are characterised by communications founded on mutual trust, by shared perceptions of the importance of safety, and by confidence in the efficacy of preventative measures" .

"The safety culture of an organisation is the product of individual and group values, attitudes, perceptions, competencies, and patterns of behavior that determine the commitment to, and the style and proficiency of, an organisation's health and safety management".

"The concept that the organisation's beliefs and attitudes, manifested in actions, policies, and procedures, affect its safety performance".

"The set of beliefs, norms, attitudes, roles, and social and technical practices that are concerned with minimising the exposure of employees, managers, customers and members of the public to conditions considered dangerous or injurious".

Safety climate has been defined as:

"Safety climate refers to a set of attributes that can be perceived about particular work organisations and which may be induced by the policies and practices that those organisations impose upon their workers and supervisors".

"The objective measurement of attitudes and perceptions toward occupational health and safety issues".

"Molar perceptions people have of their work settings".*

"A summary of molar perceptions that employees share about their work environments".*

"The shared perceptions of organisational members about their work environment and, more precisely, about their organisational safety policies".

"Safety climate is a summary concept describing the safety ethic in an organisation or workplace which is reflected in employees' beliefs about safety".

*A definition of 'molar perceptions' is 'pertaining to large units of behaviour'.

Guldenmund provides a comprehensive summary review of the range of available definitions. In comparing safety culture with safety climate he suggests that safety climate refers to the attitudes towards safety within an organisation whereas safety culture concerns the underlying beliefs and convictions of those attitudes, in other words the prevailing values of the social group. He summarises his interpretation of the available definitions as:

"'The term organisational climate was coined to refer to a global, integrating concept underlying most organisational events and processes. Nowadays, this concept is referred to by the term organisational culture whereas the term organisational climate has come to mean more and more the overt manifestation of culture within an organisation. Therefore, climate follows naturally from culture or, put another way, organisational culture expresses itself through organisational climate".

No existing research examining how organisational safety culture varies across national cultures was found during the literature survey. Multi-national organisations such as AstraZeneca, by definition, operate across several national cultures. It is not known how the organisational culture varies intra or internationally within AstraZeneca. Several functional departments may exist at any one of the AstraZeneca sites. The functions of these departments may be diverse and varied ranging from administration to manufacturing bulk drug. The presence of sub-cultures within AstraZeneca is therefore likely.

Flin et al and Cox and Flin have suggested that one set of climate indicators may not adequately describe a safety culture across different businesses. Research by Coyle et al has indicated that the organisational climate factors may not be stable over time. De Cock et al have shown that organisational culture has an element of stability over a period of at least five years.

MEASUREMENT OF CULTURE AND CLIMATE

The preceding sections have indicated that safety culture and climate are multi-dimensional and interdependent constructs. Being multi-dimensional, no one attribute may adequately describe either culture or climate. Because of the interpretative freedom, a great number of researchers have put forward methodologies by which safety culture can be measured and labelled. The majority of the organisational culture models encountered within the literature review focus on how people think, that is, their attitudes, beliefs and perceptions about specific safety climate issues. Gadd suggests that focusing on how people think may be an inappropriate approach to the investigation of safety culture as there may be differences between how people think and how they behave. Jick has suggested that, given the multi-dimensional nature of organisational culture, researchers can improve the accuracy of measuring it by the collection of several different kinds of organisational climate data.

Denzin suggests that the collection of several different types of data allows 'between (or across) methods' triangulation. Although the number of methodologies by which safety culture can be measured is great, all of the methodologies share common features. The most common administration method is via a written set of questions. The questions are sometimes the result of group discussions or interviews, these often being referred to as focus groups, in which the researchers verbally explore the issues pertinent to the particular group or organisation, (see for example Coyle et al). Sometimes the questionnaires are based upon previous research or are formulated based upon the researchers' hypotheses. The questions are usually grouped around dimensions. For example, the HSE asked questions that explored the six areas of a safety management system detailed within their guidance document HS(G)65 , namely; health and safety policies, organising for health and safety, management commitment, workforce involvement, health surveillance and promotion, health and safety audits and follow ups.

The most common type of question response format is based upon the 'Likert' scale. This requires respondents to tick one of several boxes ranging from 'strongly agree' to 'strongly disagree. The results of the survey are then generally analysed to find the structure of responses. In this structure analysis, questions responded to in a similar way suggest that they are measuring the same latent construct.

The number of latent constructs identified during structure analysis of organisational survey data varies widely from 2 to 19 . It is common for researchers to label the constructs. Examples of the latent constructs labelled by research workers, more often called 'culture dimensions', include the following:

Cabrera et al:

- Organisational emphasis on safety.
- Communication channel about safety.

- Safety level perceived on the job.
- Feedback performance on safety.
- Specific strategies for accident prevention.

Cooper and Philips:

- Management attitudes towards safety.
- Perceived level of risk.
- Effects of work pace.
- Management actions towards safety.
- Status of the Safety Officer and safety committees.
- Importance of safety training.
- Social status of safety and the promotion of it.

Glennon:

- Perceived influence of safety and health legislation.
- Perceived corporate attitude to safety and health.
- Perceived organisational status of Safety Advisory Officer.
- Perceived importance of safety and health training.
- Perceived effectiveness of encouragement (vs. discipline) in promoting safety.
- Perceived effect of departmental and section safety record on individual's promotion prospects.
- Perceived risk level of workplaces.
- Perceived status of safety targets relative to production pressures.

HSE:

- Organisational commitment.
- Line management commitment.
- Risk-taking behaviour and some contributory influences.

- Personal role.
- Workmates' influence.
- Competence.
- Supervisor's role.
- Obstacles to safe behaviour.
- Permit-to-work systems.
- Reporting of near-misses.

Guldenmund performed an extensive review of the available research in the field of safety culture, summarising about 150 safety culture factors found in the literature. Flin et al performed a thematic analysis of eighteen publicly available industrial-based safety climate surveys.

Table – The most common themes assessed in safety climate questionnaires

1 Management (13) and Supervision (4)

2 Safety System (12)

3 Risk (12)

4 Work Pressure (6)

5 Competence (6)

Management/Supervision: The perceptions of management's attitude towards safety as well as production were mentioned explicitly within 13 of the studies. The 'management' thematic label was found to be implicit in the remaining 4 studies.

Safety System: The safety theme encompassed aspects of the company's management system and included items such as: safety officials, safety committees, permit to work systems, safety policies, safety equipment.

Flin et al recognised that these safety systems may already be measured by other conventional audit procedures such as the International Safety Rating System (ISRS) and proposed that:

> *"Perception of the state of the safety systems is clearly an important component of a safety climate audit but where data on workforce perceptions are available from other measures used on site, this may not need to be included within a climate scale, allowing more attention to be devoted to other factors".*

Risk: This theme encompasses self-reporting risk taking, perceptions of risks and hazards on the worksite, and attitudes toward health and safety.

Work Pressure: The work pressure theme includes issues around the factors associated with the often precarious balance between production pressure and safety.

Competence: The competence theme hinges around the employees' perceptions regarding the recruitment of, and the skills, knowledge and experience of personnel being employed.

A set of climate factors may adequately represent elements of an organisation's safety culture. However, the same set of factors may not necessarily be able to accurately measure another organisation's safety culture. Flin et al and Cox and Flin suggest that there are insufficient empirical data on the applicability of these common thematic labels across industry or across different cultures. Coyle et al have argued that safety climate factors are not stable throughout an organisation. They administered a climate survey on two similar organisations in Australia. The organisations were involved with the provision of health care and social services to the elderly, with the greater percentage of the workforce being involved in office, nursing, and social work duties. Both organisations were members of a common church organisation. Upon examination of the results of the survey using principal component analysis, different factors and numbers of factors arose.

Organisation 1

- Maintenance and management issues.
- Company policy.
- Accountability.
- Training and management attitudes.
- Work environment.
- Policy/procedures.
- Personal authority.

Organisation 2

- Work environment.
- Personal authority.
- Training and enforcement of policy.

Funded partly by the Off-shore Safety Division of HSE, Cox and Cheyne developed a 'Safety Assessment Toolkit'. The aim of the toolkit was to enable the profiling of the safety climate within the offshore oil extraction industry. The toolkit was developed in three stages. Firstly, group discussions were held with 375 employees in 40 groups during which the participants were asked the following four questions:

- What do you understand by the term 'safety'?
- What do you understand by the term 'company culture'?
- How does safety fit into your picture of company culture?
- What do you understand by the term 'safety culture'?

In the second phase, the conversations were analysed and the number of times a particular concept occurred, such as 'attitude toward safety' and 'priority of actions over safety', was recorded. Eleven such concepts or constructs were identified. A bank of questions was then developed based upon the constructs identified in the discussion groups and upon questions contained within prior research from other industries conducted by Lee, Donald, Byrom and Corbridge and Cox and Cox. In the final phase, recipients of the questionnaire were then asked to assign a score to each question, the aggregate from all respondents then being used as an indicator of safety climate.

James and Jones proposed that three attributes should be measured by a company wishing to measure its organisational culture, namely:

- Organisational structure attribute.
- Perceptual-organisational attribute.
- Perceptual individual attribute.

The approach is similar to that suggested by Denison and Jick. Organisational structure attributes are those tangible aspects of an organisation that can be measured by audits. Perceptual-organisational attributes are those aspects of an organisation that can be seen as organisational effects. An example of an organisational effect would be the workers perceptions regarding the organisation's commitment to safety. Perceptual individual attributes are those manifestations of individuals' feelings and perceptions regarding organisational issues and their related behaviour.

Coyle et al used a different approach to develop their safety culture questionnaire. It was based on interviews with a representative cross section of personnel. In groups of ten or less, personnel were asked to anonymously write down the six most important safety issues they believed to be relevant to them in the performance of their job or that they were aware of in the organisation. All of the issues were then shared with the group. The group members then ranked each of the issues individually. The individual member rankings were then summed to give a group ranking. The top six group issues were then carried forward and used for the basis of questionnaire items.

The HSE has since 1997 promoted the use of an 'advanced software' safety climate assessment tool. The HSE write:

> *"The prime purpose of the tool is to encourage employee involvement in health and safety by seeking people's views on some key aspects of health and safety in their organisation and then involving them in seeking improvements based on the information which emerges".*

The tool consists of a 71-statement questionnaire that is issued to the workforces. The questions are responded to by choosing one of five boxes ranging from 'strongly agree' to 'strongly disagree'. Each of the survey questions is assigned to one safety culture factor. The factors were created from the analysis of the trial responses. 5,800 question responses were used to identify the following ten culture factors:

- Organisational commitment.
- Line management commitment.
- Risk-taking behaviour and some contributory influences.
- Personal role.
- Workmates' influence.
- Competence.
- Supervisor's role.
- Obstacles to safe behaviour.
- Permit-to-work systems.
- Reporting of near-misses.

Respondents are assigned to one of the following three categories:

- Workforce (those who do not have line management responsibility).
- Supervisors (those who manage the workforce).
- Management (those who manage the supervisors).

Although promoted as 'advanced software', the HSE culture software tool does nothing more than produce various graphical outputs of the response information. An example of the graphical output would be the percentage of favourable, neutral and unfavourable responses to a particular culture factor such as 'competence'. The HSE do, however, offer a benchmarking service whereby companies can compare their climate results with those of other organisations. The tool has two major flaws:

1) The tool assumes that the numbers of factors as well as the factors themselves are the same in each company. Research by Coyle et al has shown that the type and number of factors vary from organisation to organisation.
2) The tool does not give the users an indication of which factors most strongly influence safety performance.

Not withstanding the deficiencies outlined above, the use of the HSE culture survey tool will have a positive effect as it leads to an increased awareness of SHE issues amongst the workforces and is a valuable aid to managers to help focus on the key SHE issues within the organisation.

As the above literature search has shown, the number of organisational climate factors identified in previous work varies considerably. The number of climate factors identified is, in part, a direct result of the way in which the climate questionnaires were developed. In all cases the climate themes resulting from group interview, audit findings, observations etc, are derived from an individual's or team's interpretation of what themes they think are important. What is selected by the researchers is in turn influenced by the researchers' preconceptions of what is and what is not important. Coyle et al write:

"There does not seem to be any way round relying, at least in part, on safety professionals' assessment of what is important to ask, because relying on structured interviews and/or other techniques such as Delphi processes to develop questionnaire items may well result in over-inclusion of items idiosyncratic to a particular organisation. Conversely, relying on supposedly general questionnaire items will inevitably result in failure to identify factors idiosyncratic to a particular organisation, which may be important".

Various aims regarding the use of safety climate metrics have been proposed. These include:

- To reveal a safety programme's strengths and weaknesses.
- To provide an alternative to traditional safety performance indicators.

Safety culture within an organisation can be measured at several levels. Guldenmund and Schein have used a three level framework consisting of basic assumptions, espoused values and artefacts. The HSE have recently published a very brief research report that provides a five-layer model for industry to assess how mature its safety culture is. The HSE have also created guidance on how industry can improve its safety culture by use of the business excellence model. The difficulty in measuring organisational culture has been noted by Guldenmund:

"Organisational climate is commonly conceived of as a distinct configuration with limited dimensionality surveyed through self-administered questionnaires.

Such measures are, up to a certain point, objective and semi-quantitative. Organisational culture is often determined phenomenologically, i.e. through observations and interviews, through trial-and-error, mutual comparison and the like. Such measures are regarded as qualitative and thus difficult to quantify".

METRICS OF SHE PERFORMANCE

Requirement for SHE Performance Indicators

Good SHE management principles prescribe monitoring of SHE performance. Such performance monitoring requirements are included in SHE management systems guidance such as those written by the HSE and ISO. The measurement and positive response to SHE performance indicators also makes good business sense, as significant loss-prevention savings can be made.

Lagging and Leading SHE Performance Indicators

Measurement of SHE performance can be done proactively or reactively. Proactive measurements are made before an event, and reactive measurements are made after an event. Proactive measurements are often referred to as 'leading' and reactive measurements as 'lagging' indicators. Reactive measurements include the reporting of the number of injuries, accidents and loss incidents. Proactive SHE measurements include examining the number or quality of audits performed, number of 'toolbox' talks, workplace inspections and environmental performance monitoring with statistical process control.

Leading SHE performance measurements have benefits over lagging indicators in that absence of occurrence of lagging indicator occurrences does not necessarily indicate the absence of underlying problems that could give rise to a loss event. From a business and perhaps ethical standpoint it is therefore more appropriate to build SHE improvement strategies around leading SHE performance indicators. Reliable and meaningful leading indicators are, however, generally more difficult to identify, construct and manage. Further information regarding the usefulness of leading versus lagging SHE indicators is given by Mansley.

It is a generally accepted view that the majority of industries assess the success of their safety programmes using lagging indicators and that the measurements of leading indicators are rarely used as 'key performance indicators'. Lagging SHE performance indicators such as environmental incident and accident rates present a direct and unambiguous measure of safety performance. Thompson et al suggest that these lagging indicators are not effective measurements of safety for the following reasons.

- "Generally accidents and incidents occur infrequently. The resultant low variance means the statistical significance of any results is reduced".
- "Accidents do not necessarily occur to those people who are in control or who have an influence over the outcomes".
- "No matter how safe and compliant personnel are, extraneous random events and influences can cause or contribute to accidents".
- "The way in which accidents are recorded may be inconsistent. Under- and over-reporting can give rise to errors".
- "The severity of accidents may have an influence over whether an incident is or is not reported. For example, sawdust in the eye requiring eye-wash irrigation may go unreported. The surgical removal of swarf from an eye will more likely be reported".

Although the above reasons may affect the reporting of accident statistics they should not preclude their use in research as will be discussed later. The problem of using accident data such as lost time injuries in culture research has been highlighted by Zohar and Menckel and Carter, who note that lost time injury accidents occur relatively infrequently and therefore it may take many years to collate enough data to be statistically significant.

The difficulty in identification and selection of suitable SHE lagging performance indicators is well recognised in organisational safety research literature. Diaz and Cabrera write:

"In our opinion, one of the greatest challenges for organizational safety researchers is precisely the development of a set of reliable measures of organizational safety. This would imply the use of various measures, not only one".

If a statistically significant link between lagging SHE performance indicators and SHE culture factors could be shown, then the latter would form the basis of a potentially powerful leading SHE performance indicator. The identification of a link between organisational culture and lagging indicators and its subsequent use as a leading SHE KPI is one of the principal objectives of this research.

Behavioural Performance Indicators

It has been claimed that 96% of industrial accidents are caused by unsafe behaviours. Since unsafe behaviours precede accidents, their measurement provides a leading SHE performance indicator. Behavioural-based safety programmes such as Safe Unsafe Acts Auditing and B-Safe measure workers' behaviours. The scoring of behavioural audits allows for the identification of unsatisfactory behaviours as well as reinforcement of desirable behaviours. Although most behavioural safety programmes are fundamentally similar in approach, their output and scoring systems differ. Inter-comparisons between companies using two different systems are not therefore possible.

Factors Affecting the Reporting of Performance Indicators

Several factors may influence the accuracy of reported SHE performance indicators. Madsen has indicated that accidents, incidents and near misses are more likely to be reported in a supportive 'no-blame' working environment compared to an environment in which reporting is likely to give rise to punishments or other retribution. Pidgeon disagrees and suggests that a reporting culture should take into account some degree of responsibility and accountability. Safety incentive schemes can cause under-reporting of events. Safety schemes provide monetary or other rewards for good SHE performance. Rewards may be paid to individuals, groups or charities. Sawacha et al found that the introduction of bonus payments for good productivity performance reduced reported safety incidents.

Self-reported Performance Indicators

Several researchers have used self-reported accident data within their research. The use of self-reported accidents is questionable due to the following reasons:

The personnel responding to the survey may feel pressurised into answering how they think they are expected to answer. Cooper calls this effect "social desirability bias".

The accident data are not formalised and are therefore open to greater error compared with recorded data.

In terms of accident data, Thompson et al argued that self-reported injuries are preferred to "minor workplace accidents" as the latter often go under-reported. Thompson et al did however recognise that: " ... those unreported [minor workplace accidents] may be the best indicator of improving or worsening safety conditions that might eventually lead to serious injury".

Calculation of Accident Statistics

Researchers must be mindful of the different ways in which accident statistics are calculated when comparing data.

For example, accident frequency rates and incident frequency rates are commonly calculated within industry. Accident and incident rates do not measure the same thing.

The frequency rate is the number of occurrences of a given type of event expressed in relation to the base unit of measure. For example, number of accidents per number of hours an employee is at work. The formula for injury frequency rate taken from Ridley is given in Equation 1.

$$\text{Injury Frequency Rate} = \frac{\text{Total Number of Injuries in Year}}{\text{Total Number of Man Hours Worked in Year}} \times 100{,}000 \quad (1)$$

CORRELATION BETWEEN ORGANISATIONAL CULTURE AND SHE PERFORMANCE

Although safety culture has been stated to be an important contributory factor that predates accidents such as Piper Alpha and Kings Cross, little research has been done to establish the quantitative link between the two. Pidgeon noted:

> *" ... some 10 years on from Chernobyl, the existing empirical attempts to study safety culture and its relationship to organisational outcomes have remained unsystematic, fragmented, and in particular under-specified in theoretical terms".*

In his discussions regarding the evolution of the terms 'safety culture' Sorenson wrote:

"Statistical evidence that unambiguously links safety culture with the safety of operations is surprisingly rare, especially within the nuclear industry".

Industry's enthusiasm to improve safety culture in the absence of statistical evidence linking it to organisational outcomes has been summarised by Sorensen:

"The proponents of safety culture as a determinant of operational safety in the nuclear power industry are relying, at least to some degree, on that indirect assumption [that relatively low accident plant must have a relatively good safety culture]".

Even in the arguable absence of a significant statistical link between safety culture and lagging performance indicators, other researchers have commented upon the positive benefits of carrying out organisational culture climate surveys. Bailey and Peterson concluded that a safety perception survey was useful because:

- "the effectiveness of safety efforts cannot be measured by traditional procedural-engineered criteria like safety reviews, audits and inspections".
- "the effectiveness of safety efforts can be measured with surveys of employee perceptions".
- "a perception survey can effectively identify the strengths and weaknesses of elements of a safety system".
- "a perception survey can effectively identify major discrepancies in perception of program elements between hourly rated employees and levels of management".
- "a perception survey can effectively identify improvements in and deterioration of safety system elements if administered periodically".

In addition to the above, other benefits result from the administration of safety perception surveys, including:

- Raising employee's awareness of SHE issues.
- Identification of initiatives and action planning to improve SHE management systems and hardware deficiencies.
- Inter and intra-organisation benchmarking.
- Involvement of personnel in all levels of the organisation in SHE who would not otherwise be involved.
- Promotion of a positive safety climate in which SHE initiatives such as behavioural-based safety initiatives are better received and implemented.
- Raising discussion topics that would otherwise be perceived to be difficult to discuss.

In his literature review Zohar found that several organisational characteristics were able to discriminate those industrial sites with very good safety performance and those with bad safety performance. He found that the most common factor that distinguished superior safety performing sites was a strong management commitment to safety. Those sites with good safety performance were characterised by management being regularly and actively involved with safety issues. Other relationships that are more obscure were also found, for example, companies with good safety performance were characterised by personnel holding their Safety Officers in higher regard. This finding was also reported in the 1976 Accident Prevention Advisory Unit report.

Studies attempting to correlate organisational culture with lagging SHE performance indicators are complicated by the potentially very different inherent SHE risk of the units encountered. This complication results from the Heinrich et al model of accident causation. In the Heinrich et al model, accidents are caused by the simultaneous occurrence of unsafe acts and unsafe conditions. One can infer that a greater number of accidents will therefore occur in work areas with a large number of unsafe conditions compared to a similar area with a lesser number of unsafe conditions.

In his study examining the relationship between accidents and organisational culture, Zohar attempted to take the inherent risk of a workgroup into consideration by taking a risk factor into consideration which was based upon the subjective assessment of the risk each area was subjected to. Zohar failed however to establish a correlation between perceived risk of a work area and the number of accidents occurring within it.

Shannon et al performed a survey of available literature which examined the relationship between organisational and workplace factors and injury rates. Examples of organisational and workplace factors included:

- Characteristics of the workforce such as age, seniority, education, literacy.
- The presence and effectiveness of a health and safety committee such as senior management presence, numbers of workforce represented and duration of participant training.
- Managerial style and culture such as encouragement of long-term commitment of workforce, profit sharing, grievance rate, good relations between management and workers.
- Organisational philosophy on health and safety such as safety incentives, presence of rules and the unsafe behaviours of workforce observed.

Much information regarding behavioural-based safety programmes and their associations with improved safety outcomes is available in the literature. Example accounts of these systems include Ormond, Sulzer-Azaroff et al, McAffe and Winn, all of whom claim significant reduction of accident rates and business losses. The reduction of accident and loss rates claimed by proponents is significant; for example, Cooper states that a 40-75% year-on-year reduction in accident rates and accident costs represents typical improvements after the introduction of a behavioural-based management system.

Research has also indicated associations between personal characteristics and accident occurrences. Ferguson et al found a relationship between educational background and accidents. Leigh discovered a relationship between gender and accidents. Leveson and Hirchfield found a relationship between the occurrences of accidents and recent 'life events'; those having recently experienced an incident such as divorce were shown to be more likely to be involved in an accident. Melamed et al discovered a link between accidents and job satisfaction. Dwyer and Raftery have linked accidents with management reward for work rates and overtime. Cox and Cox linked perceptions of risks and/or attitudes toward safety to safety behaviour. Researching the links between safety climate factors and accidents, Coyle et al concluded that safety climate factors correlated highly with traditional (lagging) indicators. Coyle et al's experiment, however, did not quantify this correlation.

Based upon a literature review of previous research papers, Zohar formulated a safety climate questionnaire. The questionnaire consisted of 49 questions designed to measure 7 organisational climate dimensions, namely:

- Perceived management attitudes toward safety.
- Perceived effects of safe conduct on promotion.
- Perceived effects of safe conduct on social status.
- Perceived organisational status of Safety Officer.

- Perceived importance and effectiveness of safety training.
- Perceived risk level at the workplace.
- Perceived effectiveness of enforcement versus guidance in promoting safety.

The questionnaire was administered to 20 factories in the chemical, metal fabrication, food processing and textile industry sectors in Israel. The questions measuring the factors were then aggregated to give a single 'safety climate score'. A team of four judges assessed the perceived risk of each factory. Spearman rank correlation coefficients between the safety climate scores and the subjective perceived risk were calculated for 5 of the metal, 4 chemical and 3 food companies.

he resultant Spearman rank coefficients were 0.9 for the metal factories, 0.8 for the chemical factories and 0.5 for the food companies. A definition and interpretation of Spearman rank coefficient is given in Section 2.9.3.1. The usefulness of Zohar's [176] research is debateable. He did not provide any information regarding the significance of the results (although, based upon the limited number of degrees of freedom, only the metal factories' Spearman rank correlation exceeds the level of statistical significance at the 95% level). Subjective risk criteria were used and the safety climate score was one-dimensional.

Ostrom et al administered a safety climate survey within the US nuclear industry. In their paper they provided examples of the usefulness of the organisational climate survey data.

One such example given is a graphical comparison of the accident records of five departments with their relative score of one particular climate attribute. Although the comparison was made, no numerical analysis was performed.

By administration of a climate survey, Lee and Harrison measured individuals' attitudes in three nuclear power stations. 24 climate factors resulting from the climate survey were correlated with one or more of nine self-reported accident criteria. In his paper, O'Toole proposed a link between employees' perceptions of management's commitment to safety and injury frequency rate; the correlation was, however, not quantified.

Fleming et al measured subjective risk perception in six offshore drilling rigs and examined how these perceptions related to lost time accident frequency records (number of LTAs x 1,000,000/number of man hours worked) and available quantitative risk assessment data. The risk perceptions of 622 workers across six different UK oil platforms were measured by the application and analysis of a 14-section questionnaire. The risk perceptions of the workers were plotted against the rank average LTA frequency for the preceding 2-3 years. It is noted that Flemming et al did not provide the actual LTA figures within their paper. It is also noted that the use of the mean feelings for safety is questionable due to the closeness of the resultant values.

A similar study that examined the relationship between safety climate and the number of accidents was carried out at British Steel. The study correlated the attitudes of workers at sixteen British Steel plants with the numbers of accidents occurring at each plant. The study found that the correlation between safety climate and accident numbers was stronger than that between a panel of experts' perception of the inherent safety risks and accident numbers. Attempting to correlate 'feelings of safety' against accident data is potentially problematic. It is a well-established fact that individuals and groups of individuals have different thresholds of risk. Adams calls this risk threshold a person's 'risk thermostat'. What one person considers 'risky', another may consider 'acceptable'. In the absence of negative feedback, repeated exposure to risk gives rise to a person's risk tolerability threshold being raised. The consequence of this is that, for a given hazard, the correlation between feelings of risk and actual exposed risk may be weak. The use of measurements of feelings as a metric to be correlated with SHE outcomes should therefore be used cautiously.

In their paper Fleming et al also compared 'feelings of safety' with quantitative risk assessment (QRA) data. All offshore installations working within UK territorial waters are required to have a temporary refuge (TR) for emergency use. Five of the six installations provided Fleming et al with QRA data associated with temporary refuge (TR) impairment, i.e. an inability to use the refuges. Flemming et al noted within their paper that the QRA data provided to them was confidential. Fleming et al interpreted TR impairment as follows:

> *"The TR failure value is a representative measure of how secure the platform is with regard to the reliability of protective systems on the installation".*

Flemming et al proposed that the TR QRA values represented:

> *"... a measure of the cumulative failure of the systems, which takes both the probability and consequence of the events into consideration".*

The author is of the opinion that Flemming et al perhaps have an overly high expectation regarding the ability of QRA to measure the overall risk of an installation. The rankings of feelings of safety towards hazards at an installation were compared with the order of risk from the QRA calculations for TR failure. Comparison between the rankings indicated a high but non-significant correlation (due to the small sample size). Again the author questions the validity of the survey due to the closeness of the mean feelings for safety.

In a study comparing culture factors within organisations, Coyle et al wrote:

"From a proactive viewpoint, it appears that low scores on the safety climate factors identified in the organisations studied here correlated highly with traditional indices such as lost time or accident rate.

While the design of the present study did not enable this to be quantified, clearly this has major implications for planning and managing occupational health and safety. The relationship between safety climate analysis and other positive performance indicators of occupational safety and health has not been reported and is a major area for future research".

Torbjørn has examined the relationship between perceived risk, job stress and frequency of accidents and near misses. Perceived risk and job stress of eight Norwegian oil installations representing five different companies were evaluated by administering a question survey. The results of the questionnaire were analysed and compared with self-reported injury data. Although Torbjørn's study reported correlations between organisational culture factors, no statistical correlations were calculated between any of the factors and injury data.

Canter and Olearnik, Canter and Donald, Donald and Canter developed a ten factor question set to measure safety climate, and administered it to ten chemical plants in the Humberside area of the UK that operated under the Control of Industrial Major Accident Hazards (CIMAH) Regulations. The results of the study showed that there was a:

"... strong link between the ten climate measures and the number of self-reported accidents".

It is the author's opinion that the correlation of self-reported accident rates with climate metrics is inappropriate because self-reported data are unreliable. In their conclusions, Donald and Canter suggest that it would be advantageous to establish the relationship of climate factors with other safety performance indicators, especially those which are not confined to occupational safety.

Diaz and Cabrera administered a safety climate and attitude survey to two companies and one authority associated with a Spanish airport, namely:

- A ground handling division of an airline (Total workforce of 247).
- A fuel company who provided refuelling services at the airport (Total workforce of 45).
- Personnel from the airport authority (Total workforce of 73).

166 subjects participated in the survey. The responses were used to assign a safety attitude, safety climate and safety level scale to each of the three companies. The safety level scale was calculated based upon the response to six questions that measured workers perceptions regarding:

- Their involvement in an accident in the previous 12 months and the likelihood of them being involved in accidents in the near future.
- The level of safety involved with work tasks.
- The compliance with safety standards.
- The general level of safety of the operators.

Diaz and Cabrera then plotted the resulting average scores for safety attitude, safety climate and safety level of the three companies. The resultant plot indicated that high safety-level scores correlated with high safety-climate and safety-attitude scores. Although a correlation was demonstrated, the results of the analysis were not statistically significant due to only three companies being involved in the survey.

According to Zohar, establishing a correlation between organisational climate and safety outcomes has been hampered by the lack of objective safety criteria and data. Various objective criteria have been used by researchers including self-reported safety behaviour, experts' rating of safety level, retrospective accident data and frequency of micro-accidents.

Research looking at how safety climate indicators correlate with lagging safety performance indicators has been recently reported by the HSE. In their research, safety climate surveys were performed on 13 North Sea oil-drilling platforms during 1998 and 1999. In 1998, 682 questionnaires from 10 installations were available. In 1999, 806 questionnaires from 13 installations were available. The 1998 and 1999 safety climate surveys differed. Both surveys grouped questions into related themes. It is noted that the grouping of the questions into themes was done subjectively and was not subject to statistical analysis. The 1988 survey consisted of grouped questions under the following six themes:

- Health and safety policies.
- Organising for health and safety.
- Management commitment.
- Workforce involvement in health and safety.
- Health surveillance and promotion.
- Health and safety auditing.

The 1999 survey included additional questions that were grouped under the theme of operator-contractor interface.

In both surveys the average responses to all of the questions related to each theme were calculated for each installation. The resultant average responses were given the label of 'safety climate factor score'. The values of **safety** climate factor scores were then correlated with the following four lagging safety indicators:

- Number of injuries requiring absence from work greater than three days.
- Number of dangerous occurrences.
- Number of visits to the rig medic for first aid.
- Number of RIDDOR reportable incidents.

Silvia et al examined the correlation between safety climate and safety outcomes. In their study an organisational safety climate questionnaire was administered to 930 individuals, representing 40% of the population, in fifteen Portuguese organisations in different sectors, including the chemical industry, public administration, electricity and health. The responses to the survey were used to provide measures of the following five safety climate dimensions:

- Strength of organisational climate index (OCSI) (*sic*).
- Strength of safety climate index
- Strength of safety as an organisational value index
- Strength of organisational safety practices index.
- Strength of personal involvement with safety index.

Attempts to obtain accident rate, accident frequency rate and severity rate data for each of the fifteen organisations were made. Not wholly clear definitions for the three rate criteria used by Silvia et al are as follows.

Accident rate: An instantaneous bodily defect so that the individual is physically or mentally, as determined by a competent medical authority, incapable to work on a scheduled day or shift, resulting in at least three days off the job. It is noted that accident rate, as defined by Silvia et al, is actually the number of accidents that have occurred and therefore is not a rate.

The amount of time lost due to injuries per million working hours.

Severity rate: The number of workdays lost per million hours (it is noted that Silvia et al did not state in their paper that the severity rate refers to the number of workdays lost per million working hours). After examination of the collected data, Silvia et al found that not all of the 15 organisations were able to provide information that followed the above definitions. Seven organisations were able to provide accident rate data. Six organisations were able to provide accident frequency rate data and five organisations were able to provide severity rate data. Silvia et al then went on to correlate the metrics of safety climate with the above three types of accident rate data.

Table - Silvia et al Spearman correlation between safety climate metrics and accident data

Climate Factor	Accident Rate	Frequency Rate	Severity Rate
Strength of organisational climate index	(-0.865)	-0.31	-0.30
Strength of safety climate index	(-0.955)	-0.77	-0.60
Strength of safety as an organisational value index	(-0.883)	-0.77	-0.60
Strength of organisational safety practices index.	(-0.883)	(-0.83)	-0.70
Strength of personal involvement with safety index.	(-0.955)	-0.77	-0.60

Table above indicates statistically significant Spearman correlations between all five safety climate metrics **and the** accident rates. Silvia et al do not provide information regarding how many personnel were in each of the organisations taking part in the study. The author of this thesis is of the opinion that the use of accident rate as defined above, cannot be used in the above correlational exercise unless the number of personnel in each organisation is the same. This opinion is reinforced by examining the Spearman correlations between the safety climate metrics with the accident frequency rates. Column 3 of Table indicates that only the 'strength of organisational safety practices' correlates with accident frequency rates above the 95% confidence level. Zohar administered an organisational climate question survey to 534 production workers, divided into 53 work groups, in a metal-processing plant. He performed principal component analysis (PCA) on the question responses. The results of the analysis indicated two principal components which Zohar labelled as 'Supervisory Action' and 'Supervisor Expectation'. The subunit risk of each of the 53 workgroups was subjectively assessed and scored by each of the workgroup supervisors. The numbers of lost days due to injury and micro-accidents (minor accidents requiring first aid) were recorded for a period of five months following the administration of the survey. Zohar then went on to correlate subunit risk, supervisory action, supervisory expectation, injury rate (based upon micro-accidents divided by group size) and accidents (expressed as the number of lost days due to injury). The results of his inter-correlations are given in Table 2.7. In his paper, Zohar does not state what type of correlation is used. Zohar's results indicate:

- There is a marginally statistically significant relationship between micro-accidents and the number of lost days due to injury.
- There was no significant relationship between supervisory action or expectation and the number of micro-accidents or number of lost days due to injury.

Table – Zohar's correlational results

Variable		1	2	3	4	5
1	Subunit Risk	-	0.02	0.07	0.02	0.05
2	Supervisory Action		-	0.45	-0.23	0.01
3	Supervisory Expectation			-	-0.25	-0.24
4	Lost Time Injury Rate				-	0.29
5	Micro-accidents					-

In the final part of Zohar's paper he performed least squares regression of subunit risk, supervisory action, and supervisory expectation with micro-accidents as the outcome variable. Insufficient detail is provided within the paper to understand precisely what analysis was done. Zohar reported that his model accounted for 16% of the micro-accident variation seen within the responses. He went on to write:

> *'It is evident that both climate subscales provided significant prediction of the micro-accident rate'.*

For Zohar to write the above is inappropriate as his model fails to account for 84% of the observed micro-accident variation.

Zohar's use of PCA followed by regression of the resultant principal components with micro-accidents is arguably also fundamentally flawed. When PCA is applied to data, the principal components are arranged to maximise the amount of explained variance. PCA is not therefore able to take into account the correlation between the principal components and the outcome variable of interest, in this case, micro-accidents. The application of suitable statistical techniques to establish relationships between multivariate and univariate data is further explored. All of the research surveyed during the literature review that has attempted to correlate organisational culture with SHE outcomes used the mean survey responses as predictor variables. No research was found that examined the relationship between metrics associated with the distribution of the predictor variables and SHE outcomes.

According to Sorensen : "No performance indicators to gauge safety culture and its impact on safety of operations appear to have been identified and validated". After reviewing organisational safety culture and climate research over the proceeding twenty years, Guldenmund concluded:

> *" .. the measurement of safety climate could be considered an alternative safety performance indicator ... research should not be undertaken to develop 'new' safety climate measurement instruments, but should rather focus on the validity of the construct and whether it indeed yields a robust indication of an organisation's safety performance".*

Modelling of Accident Causation Factors

In an attempt to better understand the factors that cause accidents, several researchers have hypothesised the sequence and relationship of events leading up to accidents. A survey of the literature indicates that the causation factors featuring in accident causation models differ from researcher to researcher. Factors such as organisational issues, lack of personal attention, attitudes, perceptions, stress and peer pressure have all featured within accident models. According to Guldenmund there are two different types of cultural model.

- "Normative or prescriptive models which seek to describe and specify safety climate or culture per se", and;
- "Descriptive or empirical models, which attempt to summarise findings from one or several organisations studied".

According to Tomas et al, although models of accident causation are often hypothesised, they are not usually validated by the use of techniques such as structural equation modelling (SEM). Thompson et al modelled safety climate and perceptions and demonstrated that management have an important role in establishing an organisational climate that affects workplace self-reported accidents. Cheyne et al modelled employees' attitudes toward safety by relation to their appraisals of commitment to safety within their organisation. They found that:

> *" ... the architecture of attitudes to safety is, at least in part, dependent on the industrial context, or work environment. ... The models showed that perceptions of management actions and safety training were related to appraisals of the organisation's commitment to safety as well as ... to personal actions for safety".*

Tomas et al hypothesised and tested, using structural equation modelling, a seven component model of the factors that cause accidents. As well as the factors being identified, the model represents the inter-relationships between the factors. In their paper, Tomas et al also, by the use of structural equation modelling, calculated the relative strength of relationships between the factors. The model was tested on three Spanish sample groups. The number of personnel in the groups was 123, 182 and 124. The testing indicated that the model fitted two of the three samples well. The third sample was not well modelled as indicated by poor model fit indices.

Cox and Cox suggested a model of attitudes to safety based upon employees' attitudes toward four levels of objects, namely, hardware (ie safety hardware and physical hazards), software (ie rules and procedures, legislation, safety management and policy), people (ie all classes of people involved, such as workers, supervisors, management, safety committees, specialists, authorities, unions) and risks (ie risky behaviour and its regulation). According to Cox and Cox, when talking about attitudes to safety, the objects of these attitudes could always be classified into one of the four levels of objects.

After performing a review of various cultural models, Guldenmund has summarised his conclusions within a three-layer model that consists of an outer layer, middle layer and core. All of the accident models surveyed during the literature review had one common thread in that they all consider workers' attitudes and perceptions as precursors to accidents. Margolis found that workers' attitudes toward safety are directly related to managerial attitudes towards safety. The majority of the models reviewed tended to focus upon those factors directly associated with safety. It appears that research to date has paid little attention to non-safety related organisational factors such as job satisfaction, job security, and others contained within the AstraZeneca Focus 2002 survey.

The HSE developed a seven-component three-layer model of safety climate. The first layer of the model is labelled the *information exchange level* and includes three factors, namely, policy awareness, involvement and communication. The three factors in the first level measure employees' attitudes regarding health and safety information, their involvement in planning for health and safety issues and the level of direct communications about safety. The second layer of the model is labelled *central affective level* and contains two factors, namely, perceived supervisor competence and perceived management commitment. The two factors in the second level measure the attitudes of the workforce regarding the perceived competence and commitment of management. The third layer of the model is labelled *manifest and peripheral variable level* and includes two factors, namely, general safety behaviour and job satisfaction. The behavioural factor measures workers' attitudes toward issues such as procedural transgression, rule bending and taking chances. The job satisfaction factor measures the workers' attitudes regarding how satisfied they are with their job. By application of structural equation modelling, the HSE went on to establish the relative strength of the relationships between the factors within the model.

ASTRAZENECA METRICS

AstraZeneca regularly measures the attitudes and satisfactions of all its employees and the SHE performance of all of its sites.

AstraZeneca Focus Surveys

AstraZeneca recognises that employees' attitudes and satisfactions can strongly influence its ability to meet business objectives. In an attempt to measure attitudes and satisfactions, AstraZeneca has undertaken three 'Focus' surveys, conducted at two-yearly intervals commencing in 2002. The surveys were developed and administered in conjunction with an external consultancy, International Survey Research (ISR). This research uses the data generated by the 2002 survey but there was no involvement in either the design or administration of the survey itself. Previous to the research contained within this thesis, only the Focus 2000 responses have been subjected to formal analysis; in this case structural equation modelling was used to model innovative organisational climate.

Although the AstraZeneca Focus 2000 and 2002 surveys contain some common questions, the majority of them differed. At the time of writing this thesis the Focus 2004 question set and survey responses were not available to incorporate into this project. The 2002 Focus survey measured employees' attitudes, satisfactions and perceptions in ten factor areas. The mechanism by which the questions were assigned to the climate factors is unknown to AstraZeneca personnel. It is not known if factor analysis has been performed to confirm the validity of a question being allocated to a specific climate factor.

Key AstraZeneca stakeholders and ISR formulated the sixty questions covering the ten factor areas. It is noted that, although they are referred to as questions within the Focus survey, the majority of questions are in fact statements. For the purposes of this thesis, all statements and questions within the Focus 2002 survey will be referred to as questions. A number of questions are subdivided, requiring more than one response. No information, such as definitions of the wording, was provided to the respondents. AstraZeneca employees were invited to respond to the survey in work time. The survey took respondents about 15 to 20 minutes to complete.

Permitted responses to the Focus 2002 questions were as follows:

For questions 1 to 53 and 58: 1 = Agree, 2 = Tend to agree, 3 = Neither agree nor disagree, 4 = Tend to disagree, 5 = Disagree.

For questions 54 and 55: 1 = Very satisfied, 2 = Satisfied, 3 = Neither satisfied nor dissatisfied, 4 = Dissatisfied, 5 = Very dissatisfied.

For question 56: 1 = About right, 2 = Too slow, 3 = Too fast, 4 = No opinion.

For question 57: 1 = Yes, 2 = No.

For question 59: 1 = Very good, 2 = Good, 3 = Average, 4 = Poor, 5 = Very poor, 6 = No opinion.

For question 60: 1 = Yes, 2 = No, 3 = Don't know.

The Focus 2002 survey was sent to all employees via one of two methods. The first method was via the AstraZeneca intranet, the second via AstraZeneca internal mail. The method of administration chosen by a particular country was driven by the ready availability and use of company e-mail and intranet systems. The completed Focus 2002 survey responses were sent directly to the external consultancy ISR. No survey responses were held on AstraZeneca servers or databases. Personnel were not asked their names in the survey, to protect individual identities. Eight pieces of demographic data were also collected with each survey response, namely:

- In which part of AstraZeneca do you work?
- In which country do you currently work?
- Where do you work?
- In which department/team/group do you work?
- How long have you worked for AstraZeneca (including years working for Astra and Zeneca)?
- Are you male or female?
- Do you have any employees reporting to you?
- What job family best describes the nature of your work (selected from a list)?

The survey was administered to all AstraZeneca employees at all of its 53 business and operational sites around the globe. No elements of the demographic data allowed linking of a response to an individual. Responses from groups of less than 10 individuals were collated with other groups, again, to protect the identity of individuals. The survey was preceded by communications from the AstraZeneca executive team explaining the reason for the survey and how the information would be used to improve the ways of working within the company. The way in which anonymity of the survey responses would be upheld was also explained to respondents by company-wide and local communications prior to survey launch.

The 2002 survey was launched in August and was closed at the end of September. 41,720 employees participated in the survey, representing 71% of the AstraZeneca employee population.

The completed Focus 2002 response data were analysed by the ISR consultants. Part of this analysis involved comparing the AstraZeneca results with external normative values. These normative values were based upon a database of some thirty five million datasets held by ISR. AstraZeneca compared the Focus 2002 data with Focus 2000 data to help identify areas that had improved and those that required further attention. The number of respondents to the Focus 2002 data set is 45 times larger than the largest database identified during the literature review.

Only AstraZeneca personnel have participated in any of the Focus surveys to date. Appendix 3 indicates that it is common for contractor numbers to represent about one third of the total site workforce. In the case of one UK site, contractors outnumber AstraZeneca staff two to one. High proportions of contractors at any one site have the potential to influence several of the SHE performance indicators monitored. There is also a possibility that differing SHE values between contractors and AstraZeneca personnel could impact on a site's overall SHE culture.

AstraZeneca SHE performance indicators

As part of the corporate SHE management system, all operating units and marketing companies where AstraZeneca business is carried out are required to provide regular reports of their safety, health and environmental performance to AstraZeneca's Global SHE Department.

The information from the operating units and marketing companies is collated by Global SHE and is used by the business to monitor SHE performance and identify improvement opportunities. The corporate reporting procedure prescribes how accidents and incidents are reported. The procedure mandates the reporting of the following information on a quarterly basis:

The average number of AstraZeneca personnel employed during the quarter (full-time equivalents).

The number of hours worked by the AstraZeneca employees during the quarter.

The number of contractor hours worked during the quarter.

The total number of business kilometres driven during the quarter.

The number of accidents resulting in a death or serious injury (as defined within Appendix 4 of this thesis).

The number of accidents leading to damage to property resulting in business interruption.

The number of accidents leading to damage to the environment.

- The number of incidents that could have resulted in, but did not result in:
  - * An injury resulting in death or serious injury.
  - * Damage to property resulting in business interruption.
  - * Damage to the environment.
- The numbers of fires and explosions.
- The number of occupational illnesses.
- The number of external complaints by members of the public.
- The number of non-compliances with SHE licences, permits and consents.
- The number of legal sanctions.

STATISTICAL ANALYSIS OF ORGANISATIONAL CULTURE DATA

The majority of biological, mechanical, electronic and organisational systems have many inputs and outputs. The inter-relationships between the various inputs and outputs may be many and complex. These systems are classified as multivariate. Trends and relationships in multivariate data can be identified by visual examination of data tables so long as the number of variables does not exceed four or five. Although graphical representations can be of help, the ability of the human brain to identify trends and relationships in multivariate data is severely limited when the number of variables exceeds five.

The literature survey associated with measurement of organisational culture indicated that the most common method for its measurement is via attitudinal question surveys. When, in these surveys, two or more question responses correlate with one another it can be inferred that the questions may be related to the same latent factor. When selecting a statistical technique the researcher needs to be mindful of the type of data being studied. This is important, as the applicability of some statistical techniques is dependent upon whether the variables or measurements in the study are discrete or continuous.

The mean site responses calculated from the Focus 2002 and GSHE data are continuous variables. The individual Focus 2002 responses are discrete variables. As well as the type of variables, the distribution of the variables is important too. Certain statistical techniques assume specific data distributions whereas others do not. Guldenmund performed a review of current research with respect to the techniques used to analyse multivariate cultural climate surveys. He found that these tools and techniques included Factor Analysis (FA), Principal Component Analysis (PCA),

PRINCALS and HOMALAS (that latter two being computer software programs). All of the techniques are similar in that they identify intra- and inter-respondent tendencies to respond to questions, or groups of questions in a similar manner. Shannon et al performed a review of the available literature that attempted to correlate organisational and workplace factors with injury rates. Their study found that the statistical techniques used by previous researchers included:

Factor Analysis followed by Regression Analysis.

Factor Analysis followed by Discriminant Function Analysis.

Univariate analysis using sign test, Wilcoxon Matched-Pairs Signed-Rank test.

Discriminant Function Analysis, Principal Component Analysis, Logistic Regression Analysis.

t-tests.

All of the techniques identified by Guldenmund and Shannon et al are common in that they achieve one or both of the following objectives:

To understand inter-group differences and the factors that discriminate them.

To make predictions.

Techniques that address the first objective are often referred to as classification techniques. Classification allows science to simplify and hence interpret the physical world around us. An example of the usefulness of classification in the field of chemistry is the periodic table. The periodic table classifies elements into groups. Elements in each group are classified according to the way in which they are structured and react. Classification of the elements allows the prediction of the class of a previously unseen element based upon observations, or the properties of an element based upon its class. Techniques that address the second objective are often referred to as regression or correlational techniques. Regression or correlational techniques allow the identification of the relationship between predictor and predicted variables. Research question 5 requires a review of classification statistical techniques. Answers to the above research questions were achieved by:

- Identifying the statistical techniques that have been used by previous researchers to understand the structure of organisational culture and its relationship to lagging SHE performance indicators.
- Identifying the statistical techniques not previously used within the field of organisational culture that are potentially useful in answering research questions 4 and 5.

It is stressed that the purpose of this section of the literature review was to address the above research questions. The techniques were reviewed at the application level, with a view to gaining an appreciation of their applicability and limitations. A detailed examination of the mathematics supporting the techniques is therefore outside of the scope of this review.

Classification Techniques

Factor and Component Analysis

Factor Analysis (FA) belongs to a family of multiple general linear hypothesis methodologies. FA techniques can be conveniently divided into either 'exploratory' or 'confirmatory'. Exploratory Factor Analysis (EFA) is used to discover the latent structure of the data when the researcher has no previous (*a priori*) theory regarding model structure. Confirmatory Factor Analysis (CFA) is used when the researcher has *a priori* theory of the structure and relationships within the data. There are several different methods available to elucidate the latent factors within data. The two most common methods are Principal Component Analysis (PCA) and Principal Factor Analysis (PFA). Other less well-used techniques used to identify factors or components are given by Garson. PCA seeks to identify the linear combination of variables that best represents the variance. This variance is then removed and the remaining variance is then represented by a second linear combination of variables.

The process of explaining the variance and removing it is repeated until a satisfactory model is obtained. This method is called the principal axis method. The resulting model is composed of a number of orthogonal uncorrelated factors. PFA is sometimes referred to in the literature as Principal Axis Factoring (PAF) or Common Factor Analysis (CFA). PFA attempts to correlate the *common* variance of a set of variables whereas PCA attempts to elucidate a set of factors that accounts for both the common *and* unique variance. Both 'components' (from PCA) and 'factors' (from PFA) are the dimensions identified with clusters of variables. According to Garson:

> *"[PFA] represents the common variance of variables, excluding unique variance, and is thus a correlation-focused approach seeking to reproduce the inter-correlation among the variables. By comparison, components (from PCA) reflect both common and unique variance of the variables and may be seen as a variance-focused approach seeking to reproduce both the total variable variance with all components and to reproduce the correlations".*

The literature survey indicates that the use of FA is popular within the field of social sciences. Researchers, however, need to exercise caution when using FA. The variables used within the factor model can have a significant impact upon conclusions drawn. Researchers should avoid the arbitrary inclusion or deletion of factors in order to produce a good model. Results of FA are more meaningful when the researcher has a model based upon *a priori* sound theoretical judgment.

Principal Component Analysis

Principal Component Analysis (PCA) is a technique that allows simplification of multivariate data sets. The output of the analysis is a multi-dimensional model, composed of a number of variables that represent the data set. Principal component analysis is best described in terms of projections. Consider a situation where we have n objects and K variables that measure aspects of the objects. We can plot the objects and variables in a table, the rows representing the n objects, the columns representing the K variables. A K-dimensional space is then drawn and each of the objects plotted within it to form a cloud of points.

It is then possible to draw a best-fit line through the cloud of points such that the distance of all points from the line is minimised. This best-fit line is known as the first principal component (PC1). The position of each object in K space can then be projected onto the principal component line. This projection gives a new coordinate in the new coordinate system. This projection is called the 'score'. One principal component is not usually sufficient to adequately describe a data set and therefore a second component is required. The second principal component (PC2) is drawn through the mean point of the first principal component and orthogonal to it. The first and second principal components together now represent a plane in K-dimensional space. For ease of explanation assume K = 3. Figure below is a graphical representation of a two-component plane in three-dimensional space.

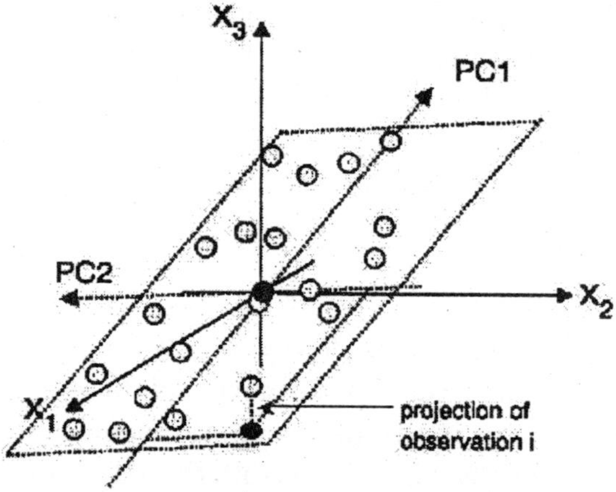

Figure – An example of a Principal Component Analysis projection from Eriksson et al

The position of any point in three-dimensional space can be projected onto this two-dimensional plane. Visualisation of this projection allows interpretation of the inter-relationships within the data. The projection is called a score plot. The score plot will be denoted by 't'. A plot of t versus t would therefore represent a score plot of the first and second principal components. Score plots may be plotted for any pair of principal components. Objects clustered together on a score plot are related to one another. Objects positioned close to the score axis indicate those that exhibit average behaviour for that particular axis principal component. Score plots are useful in identifying outliers in the data. Outliers have significant 'power' or 'leverage' to rotate the principal components towards them. Strong object outliers are detected using the Hotelling's T^2 identification tool. Hotelling's T^2 may be viewed as the multivariate equivalent of the Student's t-test and is a check for observations adhering to multivariate normality. Hotelling's T^2 is plotted on the score plot as an ellipse. The area of the ellipse corresponds to a confidence level of 95% or 99% or any other value assigned by the user.

Data points outside the Hotelling's ellipse are defined as strong outliers. In large data sets, it is expected to have a number of data points outside Hotelling's T^2 ellipse. For example, at a 95% confidence level one would expect to have 5 points outside the ellipse in every hundred data points. One can therefore assume that all of the objects adhere to multivariate distribution normality.

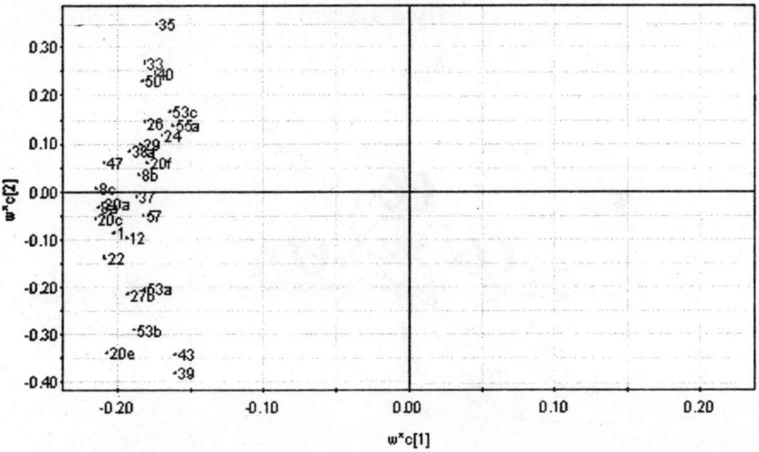

Information regarding the importance of the variables within the PCA model is obtained by examination of the loadings plot. Loadings are denoted by w^*c. A plot of w^*c versus w^*c represents a loadings plot of the first and second principal component. The further away the variable is from the loadings plot origin, the more important, or influential the variable is in the model. Referring to Figure 2.12, Eriksson et al write:

> *"Another way to understand the principal component loadings is to say that they express the orientation of the obtained model plane inside the K-dimensional variable space. The direction of PC1 in relation to the original variables is given by the cosine of the angles a_{x1}, a_{x2} and a_{x3}. Of course, another set of three*

loadings are needed to express the direction of PC2 in relation to the original variables. Hence, with two principal components and three original variables, six loading values (cosine of angles) are needed to understand how the model plane is positioned in variable space".

Figure – An example loadings scatter plot for a two-class system

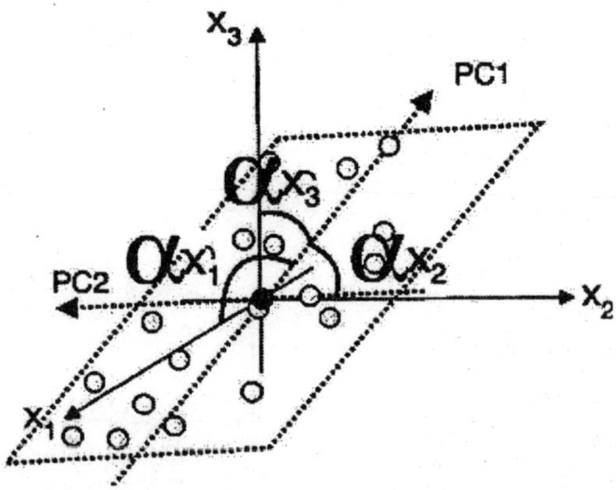

Figure – A loadings plot projection from Eriksson et al

So, if the projected PC1, PC2 principal component plane in Figure 2.12 was drawn perpendicular to X_3, variable X_3 would be found at the centre of the loadings plot. Variable X_3 would, as a result, have weak model influence. Variables X_1 and X_2 would, however, be found far from the loadings plot origin.

The distances of X_1 and X_2 from the loadings plot origin are determined by the model. The creation of PCA projections is sensitive to the scale of the variables being modelled. Variables that are more than one order of magnitude greater than the other model variables have 'strength' to rotate the projected plane toward the variable in K-dimensional variable space.

To ensure that all variables have an equal chance of contributing to the model the variables are standardised prior to calculation of the principal components. PCA software programs usually have default standardisation routines that are performed prior to the calculation of the principal components. SIMCA P+ is a software programme that performs PCA analysis. SIMCA P+, by default, performs two separate standardisation routines called 'scaling' and 'mean centering'. Scaling is achieved by calculation of the standard deviation of each of the variables. Each variable is then multiplied by the inverse of the standard deviation. Multiplication of the variable values by the inverse of the standard deviation ensures that all of the variables are given equal variance. The process of giving equal variance is sometimes referred to as auto-scaling. The process of auto-scaling prevents any one variable dominating over others due to its numerical range. Mean centering is achieved by calculation of the average value for each variable. The average values are then subtracted from each of the variables. The process of mean centring ensures that all of the variables are 'centered' around a mean value of zero. Further information regarding auto-scaling is given by Eriksson et al . Useful information can be obtained by simultaneous examination of the score and loadings plots for any two principal components.Objects in the score plot are characterised by:

- Above average responses to the variables in the same region of the loadings plot, and;
- Below average responses to the variables in the region on the opposite side of the loadings plot origin.

If the first two principal components are insufficient to adequately describe the data then a third principal component can be added to the model to improve its predictive ability. The third principal component is similar to the first two components in that it must be oriented towards the third largest variation direction within the data, be orthogonal to the other two, and be oriented to best fit the objects in the least squares sense.

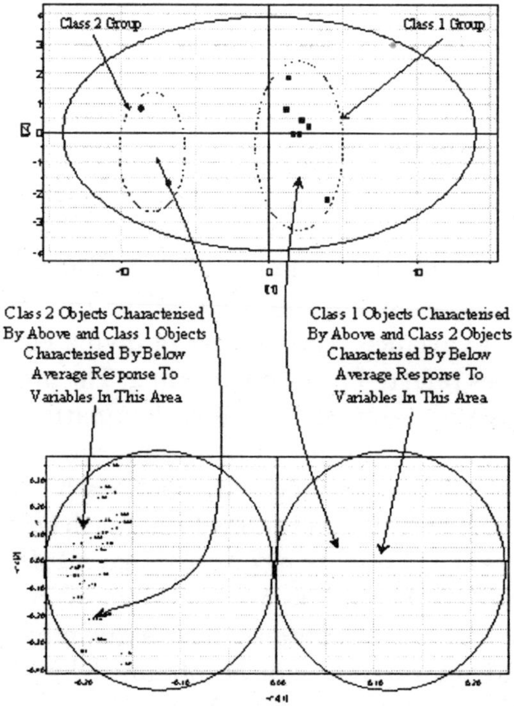

Figure – An example of how to interpret score and loadings plots

The ability of PCA to model the data is measured by a goodness of fit metric. The goodness of fit metric is denoted by 'R^2'. R^2 is a measure of the model's ability to 'reproduce the data in the training set'* (*the training set refers to the data that are used to build the PCA model). R^2 varies from 0 to 1. A value of $R^2 = 0$ indicates that the model does not fit the data at all. A value of $R^2 = 1$ indicates that the model fits the data perfectly. The goodness of fit of the resultant model increases as the number of principal components is increased. If sufficient numbers of principal components are used then the goodness of fit will approach unity. Increasing the number of principal components to achieve unity goodness of fit is counterproductive in that the resultant model may be difficult to interpret due to the large number of variables. The predictive ability of the model is denoted by 'Q^2'. Q^2 varies from 0 to 1. Q^2 is the fraction of the total variation of the data that can be explained by a principal component. A value of $Q^2 = 1$ indicates that the model is able to predict the data perfectly. A value of $Q^2 = 0$ indicates that the model is unable to predict the data. Q^2 differs from R^2 in that it does not approach unity as the number of principal components is increased.

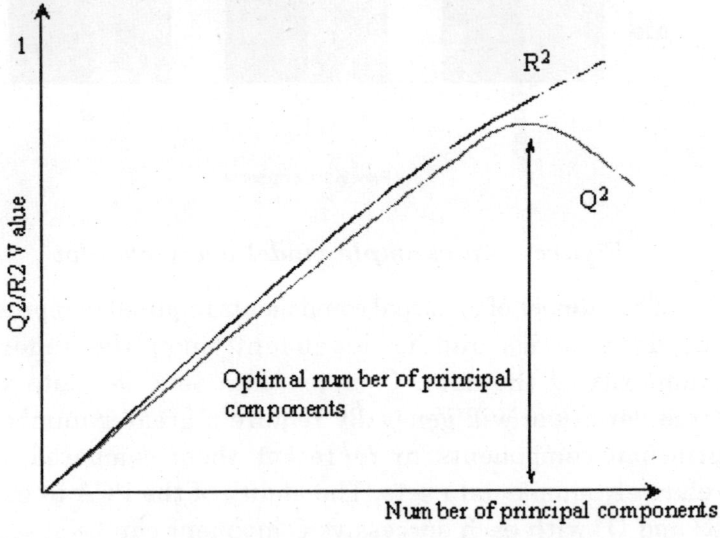

Figure – An illustration of how R^2 and Q^2 varies with increasing numbers of model principal components

The optimal number of principal components can be defined by the calculation of Q^2. Q^2 increases with the number of components up to a maximum, beyond which the predictive ability of the model does not increase. The number of principal components required is calculated from the point at which Q^2 is maximised. Figure 2.14 depicts the relationship between R^2 and Q^2. The ordinate represents the goodness of fit of R^2 and the predictive ability of Q^2. The abscissa represents the increasing complexity of the model, i.e. the number of principal components.

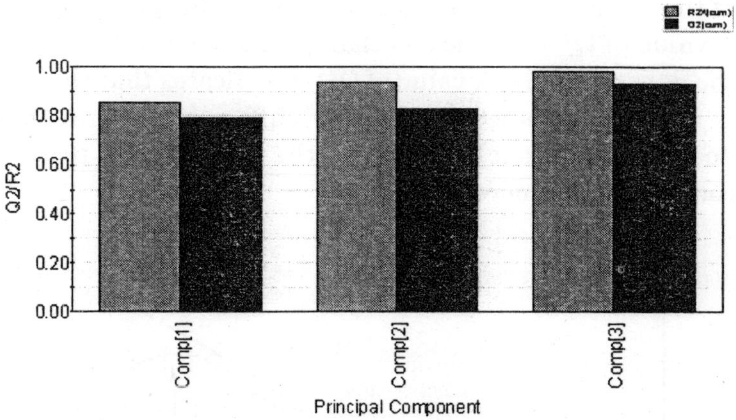

Figure – An example model overview plot

The number of principal components required to represent the data varies and is dependent upon the inherent complexity of the data. Complex data sets, i.e. data with large variation, will generally require a greater number of principal components to represent them compared with relatively simple data sets. The ability of the PCA to model R^2 and Q^2 with each successive component can be assessed by inspection of a model overview plot. The ordinate of the model overview plot represents the R^2 and Q^2 value for each component varying in all cases from 0 to 1. The abscissa of the model overview plot is the number of principal components. The model overview plot provides cumulative R^2 and Q^2 values for the model principal components. The ordinate of model overview plots is labelled Q2/R2. Q2/R2 does not indicate that Q^2 is divided by R^2. R2X(cum) and Q2(cum) in the key represents the cumulative R^2 value of the X block and model cumulative Q^2 values respectively. The plot has two main uses; firstly, it allows the researcher to view how Q^2 varies with increasing number of principal components and therefore what the optimal number of components is, and secondly, it provides information regarding how much of the variation is accounted for by each component.

According to Eriksson et al large R^2 values are required to have large values of Q^2. Ideally, the difference between Q^2 and R^2 should not be more than 0.2 to 0.3. A Q^2 value of above 0.5 should be regarded as 'good', and a Q^2 value of greater than 0.9 should be regarded as 'excellent'. They stress that these guidelines are application dependent. Further information regarding R^2 and Q^2 is given in the reference. R^2 and Q^2 may also be plotted for individual variables. R^2 Q^2 variable plots are useful in evaluating how well the variables are modelled.

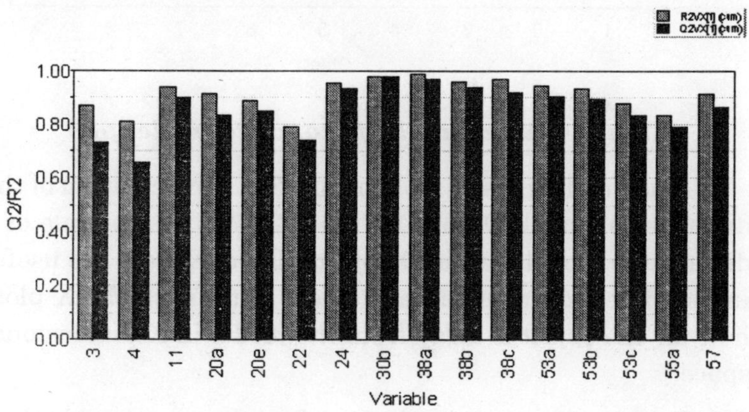

Figure – An example of an R^2 Q^2 variable plot

Those variables with poor R^2 and Q^2 values are typical candidates for deletion from the model during the model optimisation process. Figure 2.16 is an example of an R^2 Q^2 variable plot. The ordinate of R^2 Q^2 plots is labelled Q2/R2 (again, this does not indicate that Q^2 is divided by R^2). The ordinate provides the R^2 and Q^2 value for each variable. R^2 and Q^2 values vary from 0 to 1. SIMCA P+ [170] labels R^2 and Q^2 variable plots as follows: R2VX[n](cum) and Q2VX[n](cum). Where 'VX' represents 'variable'; [n] represents the nth principal component; (cum) represents cumulative. R2VX[4](cum) therefore represents the cumulative R^2 variable values for a model with 4 principal components.

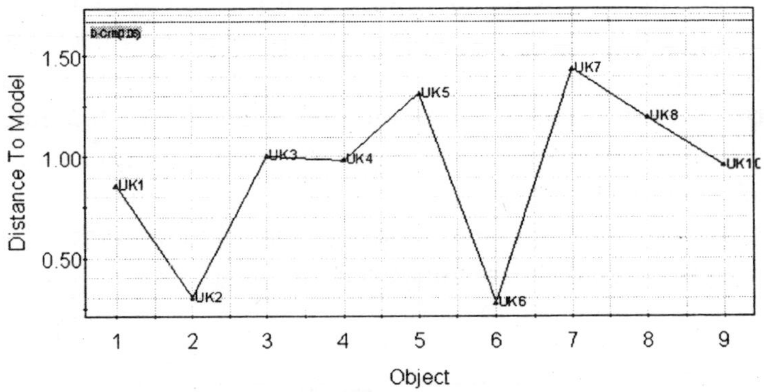

Figure – An example distance to model plot

A useful diagnostic tool within PCA is calculation of the distance to model (DModX). Figure 2.17 is an example of a distance to model plot for 9 objects. DModX plots are useful in the detection of moderate object outliers. DModX plots how far the object is away from the model in K-dimensional space.

This distance is sometimes referred to as a 'residual'. A DModX critical value is drawn on the plot. The value of DModX is determined to a confidence level selected by the researcher, normally being set at 95 or 99%. Objects that are above the critical distance to model differ, in some way that is being measured by the variables, from those objects below the critical distance to model. Figure indicates that all objects are below the critical distance to model and, therefore, no outliers exist. The ability of the distance to model plot to identify outliers is exploited in a classification technique called Soft Independent Modelling of Class Analogy (SIMCA).

Projection to Latent Structures Discriminant Analysis

When examining multivariate data, researchers may have *a priori* knowledge regarding how the objects should be grouped. In PCA the resultant model principal components are oriented to account for the maximum variation of the data. The principal components are not therefore oriented to best discriminate between the *a priori* classes. In Projection to Latent Structures Discriminant Analysis (PLS-DA) the principal components are oriented so as to account for the maximum variation in the data and, at the same time, to maximise the discrimination between the *a priori* classes. In PLS-DA a class model is built using training data of observations of known classes. New data, not previously seen by the model, can then be classified by it. An outline of the PLS-DA methodology follows. Assume that we want to build a PLS-DA model that will be used to classify previously unseen objects (people) into male or female (classes) based upon 4 continuous predictor variables. Further assume that we have a model training set of 50 males and 50 females. Assume the four continuous descriptor measurements (variables) are height, % body fat, blood testosterone and oestrogen levels for each of the 100 people in the training set. The predictor variables and classification information are entered into a table. Each row of the table represents a person (object). A person's sex (class) is indicated in the table by a 0 or 1 in columns 6 and 7. A 1 represents a person belonging to the class. A 0 represents a person who does not belong to the class.

Table – Example PLS-DA model inputs

Object	Variable 1 Height /M	Variable 2 % Body Fat	Variable 3 Concentration Of Blood Testosterone / mmol	Variable 4 Level Of Blood Oestrogen/ mmol	Class 1 (Man)	Class 2 (Woman)
1	1.2	24	14	40	0	1
2	1.3	38	19	25	0	1
---	---	---	---	---	---	---
100	1.8	27	25	25	1	0

The information within the table is then used by the PLS-DA program to create two PCA models, one model for the X data (predictor variables) and the other for the Y data (the predicted class). During the creation of the PCA X and Y data models, the principal components in each model are oriented to maximise the amount of explained X and Y block variation and, at the same time, maximise the predictive ability between the X and Y data.

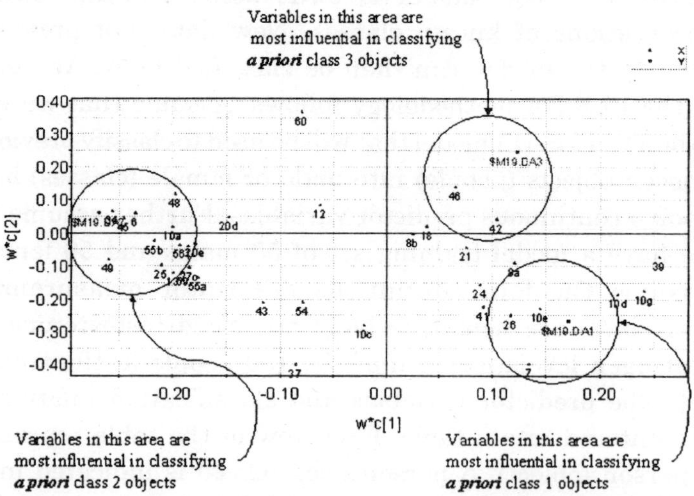

Figure – An example PLS-DA loadings scatter plot highlighting those variables that are most influential in classifying the objects

The graphical outputs of PLS-DA and their interpretation are similar to those produced by PLS. One minor difference between PLS-DA and PCA loadings plots is that the former contains *a priori* class information. In PLS-DA each *a priori* class within the model is plotted on the loadings scatter plot. SIMCA P+ assigns a symbol to each *a priori* class point using the nomenclature $MXX.DAn. $MXX represents a unique PLS-DA SIMCA P+ model number. DAn represents an *a priori* class. $M19.DA3 would therefore represent the third *a priori* class of SIMCA P+ model number 19. Variables within the loadings plot that are closest to an *a priori* class point are most influential in discriminating the *a priori* class.

Previously unseen variable data of a person (object) are plotted on the PLS-DA score plot. Classification of the previously unseen object is achieved by identification of how close the person (object) is to the *a priori* classified people within the training set PLS-DA model. Closeness of a previously unseen object to an existing class is assessed by a combination of visual inspection of the score plot and calculation of YPredPS values provided by the PLS-DA software package. YPredPS is simply the predicted Y value for an object based upon the predictor X block variables. Each object is assigned a value of YPredPS for each *a priori* class within the model. For any one class a YPredPS value close to 1 would indicate that the object is likely to belong to the class. A YPredPS value close to 0 would indicate that the object is unlikely to belong to the class. Since YPredPS is predicted by the model, actual values may be negative or greater than 1. The expected range of YPredPS values for a reasonable PLS-DA model would be between about -0.2 and 1.2. The practical application of PLS-DA is restricted to data with up to five or six *a priori* classes. The limitation of PLS-DA to five or six classes is due to the interpretive difficulties of the resultant PLS-DA score and loadings scatter plots. According to Eriksson et al PLS-DA may not be possible if the X block data do not occupy a 'tight volume in X space'. When the X block data are not tight, Eriksson et al recommend the SIMCA approach to discriminatory analysis. Further information regarding PLS-DA is given by Eriksson et al and Stahle and Wold.

Soft Independent Modelling of Class Analogy (SIMCA)

SIMCA is an approach that uses PCA as a discriminatory tool. Unlike PLS-DA, the SIMCA approach can be used when the number of classes exceeds five or six. If no *a priori* knowledge regarding possible classes is provided, then the first step of the SIMCA approach starts with PCA modelling of the entire data set. The purpose of the PCA modelling is to identify possible clusters of objects within the data. The PCA score plot identifies the clusters of objects. If *a priori* knowledge regarding potential classification of data is known, then step one of SIMCA can be omitted. Step two of SIMCA involves thc production of independent PCA class models identified in Step 1, or hypothesised by the researcher. Step 3 of SIMCA involves using the PCA models produced in SIMCA Step 2 to predict the likely classification of the observations.

SIMCA step 3 is achieved by calculating the distance an object is away from the PCA model. An example of how SIMCA step 3 classifies follows. Assume a three class system A, B and C. Further assume that three separate PCA models have been produced for each of the three classes, PCA-A, PCA-B and PCA-C. All of the objects from classes A, B and C are then entered into model PCA-A.

The distance to the model for all class A, B and C objects from model PCA-A is then plotted. The ability of model PCA-A to discriminate class A from class B and C objects is assessed by inspection of the how far the class objects are from the model. All class A objects should be below the PCA-

A critical distance to model. All class B and C objects should be above the PCA-A critical distance to model. All Class B objects should be below the PCA-B critical distance to model. All class A and C objects should be above the PCA-B critical distance to model. Finally, all class C objects should be below the PCA-C critical distance to model. All class A and B objects should be above the PCA-C critical distance to model. An alternative to plotting class information on a distance to model plot is to produce a Coomans plot. A Coomans plot allows the plotting of two PCA distance to model plots against one another. The Coomans plot creates four regions of interest::

- Objects lying in the upper right quadrant of the plot are above the critical distance for both model A and model B. Objects in this area would be classified as not belonging to either model A or model B.
- Objects in the upper left quadrant are below the model B critical distance and above the model A critical distance. Objects in this area would be classified as belonging to class B.

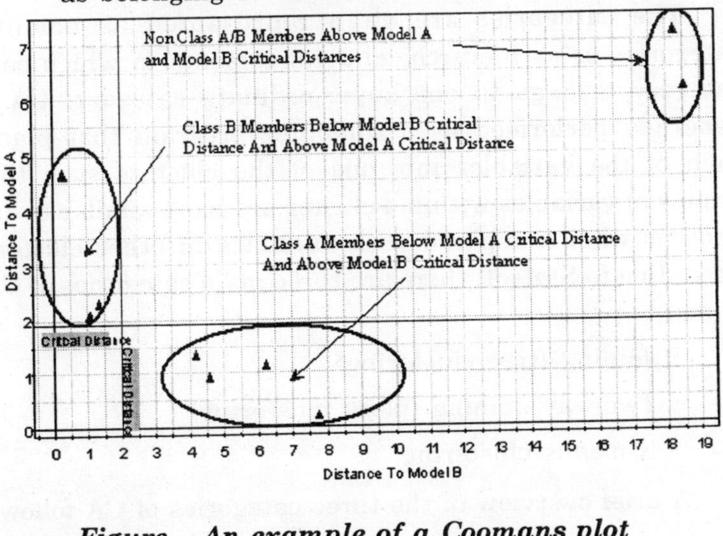

Figure – An example of a Coomans plot

- Objects in the lower left quadrant are classified as belonging to both model A and B. Objects in this area would be classified as belonging to class A and B.
- Objects in the lower right quadrant are above the model B critical distance and below the model A critical distance. Objects in this area would be classified as belonging to class A.

Cluster Analysis

The term cluster analysis (CA) was first used by Tyron to encompass a number of classification algorithms. CA is useful when a researcher is confronted by a large amount of information and needs to simplify it. According to Hammond, CA is commonly used by psychologists to explore the underlying structure of data. It has been successfully used to help diagnose mental conditions such as schizophrenia and paranoia.

The basic premise of CA is that that variables may be clustered into distinct groups. These groups of variables can be viewed as descriptive categories.

The categories are often represented as nominal categories or as hierarchical arrangements in which each category belongs to one super-ordinate category. CA is generally performed by a computer program that places each of the variables into one of the clusters such that groups of variables within a cluster are more similar to one another when compared with variables in other clusters. According to Statsoft there are three main categories of CA, namely:

- Joining (tree clustering).
- Two-way Joining (block clustering).
- K-means clustering.

A brief overview of the three categories of CA follows.

Joining (Tree Clustering) - The objective of joining (tree clustering) CA is to join objects (e.g. humans, groups of people) into successively larger clusters. The computer starts by creating a cluster for each object. The objects are then inspected and the two that are most like one another are merged to form a new object. This process is repeated until only two or more objects remain. The basis of joining two objects together is based upon dissimilarities or distance measures.

Two-way Joining - Two-way joining is the least commonly used cluster analysis technique. In two-way joining both the objects and the variables are clustered simultaneously. An example of this approach would be to cluster individuals (objects) and measures of physical fitness (variables). Two-way joining allows the clustering of individuals to detect clusters of people with similar degrees of fitness and, at the same time, cluster the variables to detect metrics that are related to group fitness.

K-Means Clustering - K-means clustering requires the researcher to provide the computer program with the number of expected clusters. The number of clusters the researcher chooses is based upon some *a priori* knowledge or hypothesis. The computer then applies the K-means clustering algorithm in order to group all of the objects into the number of pre-specified clusters. The way in which the computer allocates an object into a cluster can be seen as analysis of variance (ANOVA) in reverse. The computer starts by randomly assigning objects into one of the pre-specified clusters. The program then moves objects in and out of groups in order to get the most significant ANOVA results, i.e. to minimise the in-cluster variability.

According to Hammond, in addition to defining the number of expected clusters, one of the most significant problems associated with cluster analysis is interpretation of the resultant clusters. Because of the interpretation difficulties, cluster analysis is often seen as a precursor to more detailed analysis. For instance, the identified clusters from cluster analysis may be subjected to discriminant analysis in order to identify what factors make each cluster different. Further information regarding cluster analysis is given by Nesselroade and Cattell and Statsoft.

Support Vector Machines

Support vector machines (SVM) are a set of techniques that allow the separation of objects based upon *a priori* class membership. The way in which SVMs operate is best described pictorially. Figure represents a two-class (A and B), two-dimension case. All of the class A and class B objects are plotted in two-dimensional space. In Figure the two classes of objects are distinct, thus the SVM is able to draw a straight line between them. All class A objects are found on one side of the line. All class B objects are found on the other side of the line.

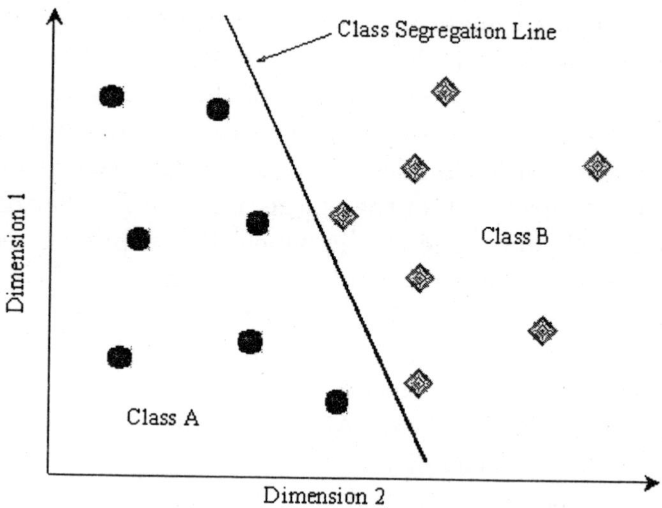

Figure – A 2-Class, 2-dimensional SVM showing distinct class membership

Figure is another example of a two-class, two-dimension case. However, in this second case, the distinction between class A and B objects is poor and instead of a straight line, the SVM is required to draw a curved line to segregate the two classes.

When SVM is applied to the data a number of kernels (calculation routines) are applied such that the separation of the two classes is maximised. Once trained, the SVM can classify previously unseen objects by the application of the kernels produced with the training set. Visualisation of how SVMs deal with data sets with more than two dimensions or more than two classes becomes difficult. In the three-dimensional, two class case, a plane is drawn to segregate the two classes.

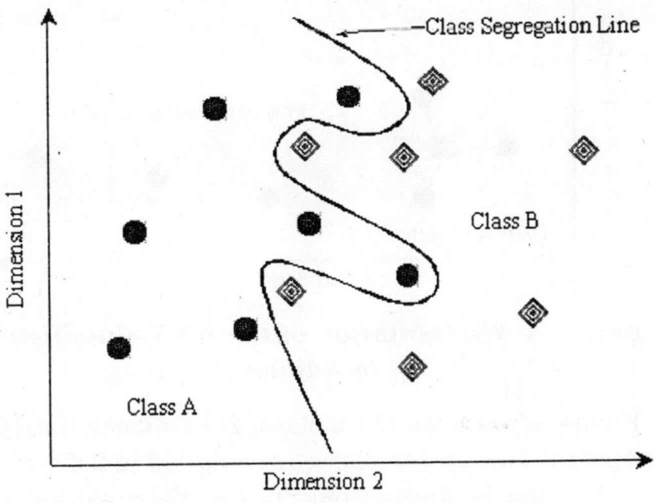

Figure – A 2-Class, 2-dimensional SVM showing indistinct class membership

If the distinction between the two classes is poor, the plane may be distorted into the third dimension. In the case of four dimensions or more, hyper-planes are drawn by the SVM to segregate the *a priori* classes. Further information, including how SVMs deal with multi-dimension, multi-class cases, is given by Christianini and Shawe-Taylor.

K-Nearest Neighbours

K-nearest neighbours (KNN) works on the fundamental principle that objects close to one another are likely to belong to the same class. In KNN a previously unclassified object is classified based upon how close it is to an object or objects of known classification.

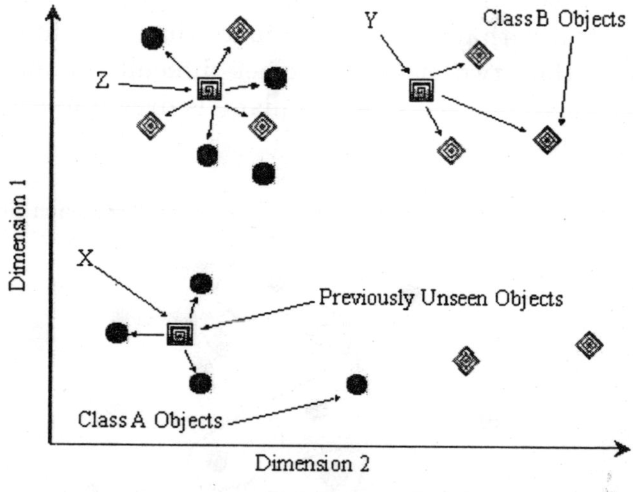

Figure – A representation of the KNN classification technique

Figure represents the 2-class, 2-dimensional case. The objects of the two *a priori* classes are plotted in 2-dimensional space. Previously unseen objects are then plotted in the same 2-dimensional space.

The previously unseen objects are then classified by assessing how close they are to their nearest neighbours. The researcher sets the number of nearest neighbours taken into account in the classification process. If the number of nearest neighbours is greater than 1 then a voting system is used.

Assuming that the researcher set the number of nearest neighbours to 3, the following classifications would result. Object X would be classified as belonging to class A due to its 3 nearest neighbours belonging to class A. Object Y would be classified as belonging to class B due to its 3 nearest neighbours belonging to class B. With the nearest neighbours set to 3, KNN could not classify object Z. Object Z would, however, be classified as belonging to class A if the number of nearest neighbours was increased to 4.

KNN can readily cope with more than two dimensions. All objects are plotted in K-dimensional space. In this case K is equal to the number of dimensions describing the objects.

The challenge in using KNN is to decide how many neighbours should be taken into account. Smaller numbers of nearest neighbours will give rise to a large variation in prediction ability. Large numbers of nearest neighbours may give rise to significant model biases. KNN computer programs can provide an estimate of a suitable number of neighbours to use.

The way in which this is accomplished is by the application of an algorithm known as cross-validation. The principal advantage of KNN over other classification techniques is that it does not require large training sets. Further information regarding KNN is given by Statsoft and Bishop.

Classification Trees

Classification trees are used to predict class membership of objects or cases based upon the measurements of one or more predictor variables. According to Statsoft, classification trees are useful as an exploratory technique, or as a last resort when traditional methods fail. According to Breiman et al, classification trees have been successfully used in medicine to help identify those heart attack victims who are most at risk after a heart attack. In Breiman's study the classification tree was based upon three factors, namely:

> *"If the patient's minimum systolic blood pressurè over the initial 24 hour period is greater than 91, then if the patient's age is over 62.5 years, then if the patient displays sinus tachycardia then and only then is the patient predicted not to survive for at least 30 days".*

The classification tree approach is similar to, but distinct from, linear discriminant analysis. Unlike discriminant analysis, classification trees classify based upon the sequential application of criteria. Using the above case to exemplify the classification tree approach; the criteria would be applied in the following order, blood pressure greater than 91 mm Hg, followed by age greater than 62.5 years, and finally, the presence of tachycardia. This is compared to the linear discriminant analysis approach in which all three factors are simultaneously applied to perform the classification. A distinctive feature of classification trees is their ability to deal with continuous as well as categorical variables. A categorical variable indicates if an object is a member of a category or not. For instance, in the above example, blood pressure and the patient's age are continuous variables, whereas the presence of tachycardia is a categorical variable. Another advantage of classification trees is they can deal with non-parametric data. Further information regarding classification trees is given by Statsoft and Dobra.

Structural Equation Modelling

The literature review indicated that Structural Equation Modelling (SEM) is a popular technique in the field of social and behavioural science. SEM is a multivariate analysis method that allows the modelling and testing of inter-relationships between hypothesised latent constructs and how these constructs are correlated with observable indicators. According to Hox, researchers most often use SEM as a confirmatory rather than exploratory technique. SEM can be differentiated from 'classical' general linear regression models such as regression analysis, analysis of variance and analysis of covariance. The main feature of SEM not found in classical regression analysis is its ability to explicitly take into account the errors associated with measurement error (not described here). In classical general linear regression models the observable data are fitted without taking errors in the measurement of observable indicators into account.

Two different types of variables are entered into structural equation models, namely, observed and latent. Observed, sometimes labelled manifest, variables are those variables that are measured by the researcher. Examples of observed variables are the responses to the Focus 2002 questions and injury rate data. Latent variables are those variables that cannot be measured directly. An example of a latent social science variable is intelligence. Intelligence cannot be directly measured; instead, inferences regarding intelligence are made from the observable indicators of intelligence such as the results from intelligence quotient tests.

The use of a single observed indicator to measure a single latent construct is undesirable since the former may contain measurement inaccuracies and can only measure a single aspect of a construct. According to Raykov and Marcoulides, latent constructs should be measured by the use of several, and at least two, observable indicators. The measurement of several observable indicators allows more reliable estimates of latent constructs to be made. The observed and latent variables are further classified as either 'dependent' or 'independent'. Dependent constructs are caused or endogenous. Independent constructs are causal or explanatory.

Further information regarding SEM definitions is given by Scientific Software International. The structural equation model has two parts, a structural part and a measurement part. The theoretical constructs and the relationship between them constitute the structural part of the model. The relationship between the measured indicators and the constructs forms the measurement part of the model. In order to test the conceptual model the structural and measurement parts must be formulated as a statistical model. The structural part of the model is most often represented diagrammatically as a path diagram.

The elements represented in path diagrams use standard symbols. The researcher starts by drawing a path diagram that indicates the relationships between the model variables. The path diagram is based upon an existing theory or a hypothesis regarding the relationships between the variables. A unidirectional arrow from one variable to another indicates that the variable at the arrowhead is caused by, or is dependent upon, the variable at the start of the arrow. Variables on the receiving end of a unidirectional arrow are called dependent variables. Variables with unidirectional arrows emanating from them are called independent variables.

Bi-directional arrows linking two variables indicate an association between the variables that has no causal relationship. Bi-directional arrows can only link two independent variables. Dependent variables cannot be linked by bi-directional arrows.

The measurement part of the structural equation model usually takes the form of a matrix of co-variances between all of the observed variables. Once the structural and measurement parts of the model have been assembled, the structural equation part of the model can be built. An explanation of the detailed mathematics associated with building a structural equation model is outside the scope of this project. Although the mathematics associated with SEM is complex, the key concepts behind the methodology are relatively easy to understand, and are as follows:

Using the programming language specific to the chosen software being used, the researcher represents the path diagram as a set of model definition equations.

The SEM program reduces the model definition equations into a reproduced covariance matrix. The reproduced covariance matrix has an entry for each of the observed indicators.

For every entry in the reproduced covariance matrix, there is a counterpart in the measurement co-variance matrix part of the model input.

The SEM program then performs a number of routines in which it attempts to minimise the difference between the reproduced and measurement co-variance matrices.

How close the reproduced and measurement co-variance matrices are to one another is signified by a fit function that is typically denoted as *F*. *F* is always equal to zero or a non-negative number. An *F* value of zero indicates that the reproduced and measurement co-variance matrices are identical. Having identical reproduced and measurement matrices means that observed variable data support the relationship between the variables that was hypothesised in the path diagram.

A good *F* value does not necessarily mean that the proposed structure is the 'true' model that explains the actual relationship between latent and observed variables; rather, it indicates that the model is a possible explanation of the observed data. There may be several other, perhaps better, models that explain the variance within the observed data. In this respect, SEM differs from classical modelling techniques where the researcher is interested in rejecting the null hypothesis. In SEM the researcher is interested in finding a model that is not rejected by the observed variables.

Once the model is completed it can be statistically tested. Relationships within the model that do not fit well are identified using the Lagrange Multiplier Test. The significance of relationships between factors is calculated by performing the Wald test. The model may be optimised by an iterative process of model postulation and testing via Lagrange and Wald tests. Further information regarding SEM model testing is given by Statsoft.

The final model will not define the exact deterministic relationships between the constructs. This is because the independent constructs within the model account for only a part of the variation within the dependent constructs. Several variables may be associated with the dependent variables that are not included within the model.

The unaccounted variables are represented by stochastic error terms, one for each construct. One fundamental assumption within SEM is that the error term in each relationship is uncorrelated with other independent constructs. Inadequately designed experiments and theoretical models will give rise to omitted variable bias, which in turn, will lead to inconsistent and biased structural coefficients. Further information regarding SEM methodologies is given by Raykov and Marcoulides.

Before correlating a latent construct with other factors it is important to test the reliability with which the set of observed variables measures a latent construct. Cronbach's alpha is a numerical coefficient of reliability of such scales. Cronbach's alpha is an index of reliability associated with the variation accounted for by the true score of the underlying construct. Cronbach's alpha values vary from 0 to 1. The higher the Cronbach alpha coefficient, the more reliable the scale is. According to Nunnaly, a Cronbach alpha coefficient of 0.7 is an indication of acceptable reliability of scale.

The way in which Cronbach's alpha is typically used is as follows. The researcher hypothesises a relationship between a set of observed variables and an underlying construct. Computer statistical software programs such as SAS® are then used to calculate an overall scale and observed variable alpha coefficients. High observed variable alpha scores indicate those variables that, if removed from the scale, would best increase the overall alpha.

By an iterative process of inclusion and exclusion of construct indicator variables followed by re-calculation of alpha, the researcher can formulate a list of observed variables that reliably measure the underlying latent construct. Further information regarding the calculation and use of Cronbach's alpha is given by Reynaldo and Santos.

Due to the complexity of SEM mathematics, the use of a computer to perform the calculations is essential.

There are many commercially available SEM comuter programs including SAS®, LISREL, AMOS, SEPATH and EQS. All of the programs appear to perform the same basic functions. The significant difference between them appears to be the way in which the researcher interfaces with the program. All of the programs require the researcher to learn a program-specific command language to use them.

Reading a selection of SEM program reviews on the internet indicated that each has a strong following. It would appear that for every person advocating the use of one program, there is another saying that an alternative is better. The current availability of a program and the support of knowledgeable colleagues may strongly influence the ultimate selection of SEM software.

Artificial Neural Networks

Artificial neural networks (ANNs) have been successfully applied in a large number of predictive applications. ANNs are particularly useful in modelling non-linear, complex functions involving many variables. Examples of the successful application of ANNs include:

- Vehicular management systems where engine and suspension characteristics are varied dependent upon the feedback from an array of transducers placed within the vehicle.
- Stock market predictions where past performance data, such as various world markets, oil price and other factors, are used to predict, in real time, future stock market performance.
- Credit risk ranking, where many factors relating to an individual, such as age, job role, marital status, income and incidents of past loan problems, are used to assess an individual's credit rating.

Two benefits of ANNs are that the user does not need to have an understanding of the heuristic structure of the data and, according to Statsoft, they require less user knowledge than other linear multivariate methods such as PCA. ANNs require training before they can be used to classify previously unseen data. ANNs are either trained using 'supervised' or 'unsupervised' learning. In supervised learning the user compiles a data set and invokes a training algorithm.

The most common training algorithm is called 'back propagation'. The program then learns the associations between the inputs and the expected outputs. In unsupervised learning the ANN learns to pick out trends within data without external influences. Unsupervised learning ANNs can be useful in reducing the dimensions of a multi-dimensional input.

The relationship between the inputs and outputs of a trained ANN is represented by a neural structure and synapse weightings. The neural structure is the number, arrangement and interconnection of neurons. The synapse weightings are mathematical functions that determine the relationship between neuron inputs and outputs.

Once trained, the ANN can be used to predict outcomes from data sets that it has previously not encountered (subject to the previously unseen data set falling within the scope of the training data set). Further information regarding ANNs is given by Statsoft and Smith . Despite the potential usefulness, no examples of the application of ANNs in the field of organisational culture and climate research were found during the literature survey.

Multi-Dimensional Scaling

According to Statsoft, multi-dimensional scaling (MDS) can be viewed as an alternative to factor analysis (FA). The goal of MDS is similar to FA in that it attempts to identify and explain the underlying differences or similarities between several objects. As for FA, MDS plots the observations in K-dimensional space where similar objects tend to cluster around one another. The ability of the MDS model to explain the variance within the data increases with the number of dimensions. The number of factors within the model may theoretically be the same as the number of observations; this, however, would be counter-productive as the purpose of MDS is to simplify the data, not reproduce it in another form. The difference between actual versus MDS-model-predicted values is calculated by a 'stress test'. The stress test can be a useful measure to help decide how many dimensions are required to represent the data. The optimum number of components is achieved at the point at which the numerical value of the stress test does not significantly decrease with the addition of another component.

MDS differs significantly from FA in that the latter requires the data to be approximately normally distributed and the relationships between the data to be linear. MDS is not dependent upon the distribution of the data or the relationships within it. According to Statsoft, FA tends to extract more factors than MDS. MDS therefore tends to give rise to solutions that are more interpretable than FA. Further information regarding MDS and model fit parameters is given by Statsoft.

Correlational Techniques

Bivariate and Multivariate Regression

In bivariate regression (BR) there is one predictor and one observed variable. The predictor variable is plotted against the observed variable. A best-fit line is then drawn through the points. The best-fit line is drawn to minimise the sum of squared distances from all of the points to the line. The shape of the best-fit line is dependent upon the relationship between the predictor and observed variable and can be represented by an equation. This equation can then be used to predict the observed variable from the measurement of a predictor variable. The strength of relationships between predictor and observed variables can be calculated using Pearson or Spearman correlation tests. Both tests result in the production of a correlation coefficient ranging from –1 to +1. A correlation coefficient of 0 indicates that the two pairs of data are not correlated with one another. A value of +1 or –1 indicates that the two pairs of data are perfectly correlated. Negative correlation coefficients indicate an inverse relationship between the two variables. The Pearson correlation coefficient is termed a parametric method. Its application is reliant upon the data being approximately normally distributed. The Pearson correlation coefficient should not be used if the data are not approximately normally distributed or if the relationship between the two variables is not approximately linear. Further information regarding the calculation of the Pearson correlation coefficient is given by Lane.

The non-parametric alternative to the Pearson coefficient is the Spearman correlation coefficient, sometimes referred to as Spearman rank correlation or Spearman rho (r). Being a non-parametric method the calculation of the Spearman coefficient is not reliant upon the data being approximately normally distributed. The literature review found several research papers that quoted correlation coefficients without providing information regarding the statistical significance of the results. The statistical significance of Pearson and Spearman correlation coefficients is dependent upon the sample size. The Student's t test is related to the Pearson or Spearman correlation coefficient (r) by Equation 2.

$$t = r\sqrt{\frac{n-2}{1-r^2}} \quad (2)$$

Here, n is the number of degrees of freedom. Calculated values can be compared to values contained within Student's t test tables, such as those found in Statsoft and Micro. In conjunction with Student's t test tables, Equation 2 can be used to calculate the critical value of the Pearson and Spearman correlation coefficients. Pearson or Spearman correlation coefficients above the critical value indicate that the relationship between the variables of interest is above a level that could have occurred purely by chance (at the level of confidence chosen). The traditional way of analysing relationships within large data tables has been the one variable at a time (OVAT) method. In OVAT an understanding of the distribution of each of the variables is gained by, for example, calculation of standard deviations, means etc. The second step is to hypothesise and test the relationships between any two of the variables.

This step is repeated for each of the variable pairs of interest. Apart from being considerably labour intensive, the OVAT method suffers a significant problem.

At the 95% confidence level the risk of the researcher finding a false positive (or negative) relationship between two variables is 5%. Equation 3 gives the relationship between the probability of a false relationship, for a 95% confidence level, and the number of variables

probability = $1 - 0.95^{n}$ (3)

where n is the number of variables. Table below indicates how the probability of a false relationship approaches unity when n becomes large.

Table – Probability of a false correlation with increasing n

n	**Probability at 95% confidence level**
10	0.4013
60	0.9539
100	0.9941
150	0.9995

The only way to circumvent this problem of error is to analyse all of the variables simultaneously. It is noted that the Focus 2002 survey contains 81 questions.

Based upon Equation 3, using an OVAT approach on this data set, one would anticipate seeing about 3 or 4 false relationships at a 95% confidence level. In multivariate regression (MR) there are several predictor variables and one observed variable. Equation 4 can represent the relationship between the observed and predictor variables, in the case of a linear relationship.

$$Y=a + (\beta_1 \times X_1) + (\beta_2 \times X_2) + ... + (\beta_n \times X_n) \qquad (4)$$

where:

Y is the observed variable.

a is a scaling factor.

β_n is a Beta factor for the nth predictor variable.

X_n is the nth predictor variable.

The Beta factors indicate the importance the variable in being able to predict Y. Large Beta values indicate greater importance of the predictor variable. The scaling and beta factors are calculated so as to best approximate Y. According to Hammond, the accuracy of multivariate regression decreases when the predictor variables are highly correlated with one another.

This problem is referred to as multi-colinearity and arises due to problems associated with estimation of the beta values. Techniques such as 'ridge estimation' or 'Stein estimation' methods are available to circumvent the problem. According to Hammond, multivariate regression should be avoided when the predictor variables are highly correlated.

Projection to Latent Structures by partial least squares

Projection to latent structures by partial least squares (PLS) is a method that enables the identification of linear relationships between two separate data sets X and Y. Data set X may be composed of sets of known observations or predictor variables.

Data set Y may be composed of observations such as chemical reaction yield, quality etc. The number of predictor and predicted variables in the X and Y data blocks is limited only by the size of the data sets. According to Eriksson et al, PLS has been successfully applied in the fields of computational chemistry, quantitative structure-activity relationships modelling, multivariate calibration and process monitoring and optimisation. As for PCA, PLS is best envisaged in graphical terms. The predictor variables of the X data block are plotted in K-dimensional space.

The predicted variables in the Y data block are plotted in M-dimensional space. Every object has a predictor variable in K-dimensional space with an associated predicted variable in M-dimensional space. The n points of the X and Y data blocks are represented by a best-fit principal component line. The X data principal component line is plotted in K-dimensional space.

The Y data principal component line is plotted in M dimensional space. At the same time the principal component lines within K and M dimensional space are oriented to best approximate the relationship between the X and Y data. In PLS, principal components in X dimensional space are denoted by t. Principal components in Y dimensional space are denoted by u. The term t_1 therefore denotes the first principal component of X dimensional space, u_1 denotes the first principal component of Y dimensional space. The resultant model is represented as two best-fit lines in two different dimensional spaces, the association between the lines being representative of the associations within the X and Y data. As for PCA, one principal component is often insufficient to adequately represent the data. Additional principal components are added in order to increase the model's ability to account for the variance.

How well the model is able to represent the data is dependent upon the association between the X and Y data. The stronger the relationship between the X and Y data blocks, the better the model will be able to represent the data. PLS is a parametric method. It assumes that both the X and Y data blocks are approximately normally distributed. According to Eriksson et al, PLS works best when the data are fairly symmetrically distributed and have a fairly constant error variance. The requirement for constant error variance means that variables that range more than a factor of 10 require logarithmic transformation prior to analysis. Non-normal distributions of either X and Y block require transformation prior to PLS analysis. PLS also requires the relationship between X and Y data to be linear. PLS computer software packages, such as SIMCA P+ , have diagnostic tools that allow the identification and transformation of non-linear relationships between the X and Y data blocks.

As for PCA, PLS can be performed by manual calculation. The use of software packages such as SIMCA P+ to perform PCA and PLS is preferable to manual calculation. In addition to substantial time savings, these packages offer additional functionality that includes distribution transformations as well as pre- and post-analysis processing that allows non-linear relationships to be successfully modelled. Further information regarding non-linear PLS modelling can be found in Hoskuldsson and Wold et al. PLS model graphical outputs include score, loadings, distance to model and R^2, Q^2 plots, and are similar to those produced by PCA. PCA, however, only has to account for an X data block, whereas PLS models have to account for X and Y data blocks. PLS models therefore produce additional metrics to indicate how well they are able to account for the Y block variation and predict Y values. The terms used in PLS to describe the Y block are similar to those used to describe the X block in PCA. Therefore, R^2X represents the model's ability to account for the X block variation. R^2Y represents the model's ability to account for the Y block variation. An additional diagnostic tool used in PLS, but not found in PCA, is a variable importance plot (VIP).

A simplistic description of variable importance is the square of the model's variable loading, for all model principal components, multiplied by the percentage of explained variable variation. So, variables with low loading or those that cannot be predicted well by the model, or both, are assigned a low variable importance. Variables with high loadings or those that are well explained by the model, or both, are assigned higher variable importance. The mathematics associated with the calculation of variable importance is outside the scope of this literature review. Further information is given by Eriksson et al. The VIP is useful in the identification of those variables that are most and least influential in the model. The variables in the VIP are usually arranged in order of model importance. Those variables with higher VIP values are more influential in the model than those variables with low VIP values. The 'high-low' error bars drawn upon each variable column indicate the degree of variable variance. The confidence limit of the error bars is selected by the user and is usually set to 95%. Variables with large error bars give rise to undesired model variance that in turn gives rise to poorer overall model R^2 and Q^2 values. Inspection of the VIP often shows a number of steps in the values between variable importance. During the model optimisation process, it is common practice to delete the following variables during PCA and PLS model optimisation:

- Variables to the right of a 'step'.
- Variables with a VIP of less than 0.8.
- Variables with large VIP error bars.

Prior to the use of PLS and PCA it is common to pre-treat the data in order to simplify the predictor data. One method of pre-treatment is orthogonal signal correction (OSC). According to Eriksson et al, OSC was originally developed to filter non-informative data from laboratory analytical chemistry spectra. The application of OSC prior to modelling can improve the predictive ability of a PLS model. The combination of PLS with OSC-corrected data is referred to as PLS-OSC. A detailed explanation of the matrix algebra associated with PLS-OSC and the various algorithms used to produce it are outside the scope of this literature review. Further information is given by Eriksson et al.

A simplistic overview of the principles of PLS-OSC is as follows. Within a PLS model there may be some X block data that do not correlate well with the Y block data. Because the PLS model principal components are oriented to account for both the correlated and uncorrelated X data, the predictive power of the PLS model is reduced. The process of PLS-OSC is achieved by orienting the X and Y block principal components such that the correlation between the X and Y data blocks is maximised and, at the same time, an orthogonal vector from the first principal component X block vector is drawn. An algorithm called NIPALS is applied to the data in order to reduce the variance of the X block data in the orthogonal vector. The resultant PLS-OSC model now only represents the variance in the X block data that is correlated with the Y block data. As less X block information is represented in the PLS-OSC model, the predictive power is increased compared with a PLS model. Other PLS pre-processing and data simplification techniques are available to researchers. These techniques include multiplicative signal correction (MSC) and standard normal variate (SNV) correction methodologies. Further information regarding MSC and SNV is given by Eriksson et al [53] . The building of PLS models has been described by regular practioners as an art as well as a science. Two independent researchers given the same X and Y data are unlikely to produce identical PLS models. The reason for the differences can be explained by the iterative nature of PLS modelling. Competent PLS practioners will define a modelling strategy that will be based along the following outline steps.

Step 1) Examination of univariate statistics and data pre-treatment - The reason for examination of univariate statistics is to attempt to gain an *a priori* understanding of the data structure prior to modelling. The creation of simple distribution histograms and, for example, Pearson correlation matrices may inform the researcher of trends and relationships within the data that may subsequently influence decisions in the modelling process. The examination of the data will generally indicate whether the data are required to be pre-treated. Pre-treatment of data may include log transformations to produce distributions that are closer to normality.

PCA is generally performed prior to PLS analysis. PCA further helps to identify relationships within the data. The various PCA model outputs also aid in the identification of outliers and clusters of data that may be removed prior to PLS modelling. The presence of clusters may hinder the predictive ability of a model. Clusters are generally removed and modelled separately to better understand their structure.

Step 3) Model validation - Once a PLS model has been built it is important to assess its validity. A valid model is able to predict Y data better than chance. Within PLS there are three principal methods by which the validity of a model may be assessed, namely:

External validation,

Internal validation (cross-validation),

Response permutation validation.

The three validation methodologies are briefly described below. Further detailed information regarding PLS model validation is given by Eriksson et al.

External validation: External model validation is generally the preferred method of validation. In external validation the model is validated by using independent data that have not been part of the training data set. The validation X block data must be representative and must fall within the span of the original model training data set. The validity of the PLS model can then be assessed by running the validation data set through the model and comparing the predicted Y information with actual Y values. One disadvantage of the external validation methodology is that it requires a large number of X and Y data points if it is to be statistically significant.

Internal cross validation: Internal cross validation is performed by randomly splitting the data into two separate training blocks. A separate PLS model is then built for each data block. The X block data used to train the second model are then entered into the first model, and the X block data used to train the first model are entered into the second model. Both models are run separately and the differences between the predicted versus real Y values are calculated. The predictive residual sum of squares, which is a measure of the predictive ability of the model, is then calculated. As for external validation, internal cross validation requires a large set of X and Y data to allow the building of two training blocks.

Response permutation validation: SIMCA P+ [170] has a built-in validation function. When the response permutation validation function is initiated, the X block is left intact whilst the Y block is randomly re-ordered. A new PLS model is computed for the re-ordered data and corresponding values of Q^2 and R^2Y are calculated. Values of Q^2 and R^2Y from the original model are compared with those of the re-ordered model. If the original model results occurred by chance then one would expect the re-ordered Q^2 and R^2Y values to be close to the original model Q^2 and R^2Y values. If the original model results are valid, i.e. not created by chance, one would expect the values of Q^2 and R^2Y of the re-ordered models to be significantly less than the original model Q^2 and R^2Y values. This process of re-ordering of the Y block and recalculation of Q^2 and R^2Y is repeated a number of times (set by the SIMCA P+ user up to a value of 999).

For each permutation the Pearson correlation coefficient is calculated between the original and the permuted Y data. If the process of re-ordering does not significantly perturb the model then the Pearson correlation coefficient will be close to unity. If the process of re-ordering the Y block gives rise to a large difference between the original and permuted value then the Pearson correlation coefficient will approach zero. Figure 2.26 is an example of a response permutation validation plot. Q^2 and R^2Y are plotted against the Pearson correlation coefficient for each of the re-ordered models and a best-fit line drawn through the set of Q^2 and R^2Y values. The ordinates of response permutation validation plots are labelled Q2/R2. The labelled ordinate represents R^2Y and Q^2 and not Q^2 divided by R^2Y. According to Eriksson et al a valid model has a R^2Y ordinate intercept no greater than 0.3 to 0.4 and the Q^2 intercept should not exceed 0.05. These values should only be used as a guide. This is particularly the case when the number of objects studied is less than ten. According to Ellett the R^2Y ordinate intercept value is unimportant so long as the Q^2 ordinate intercept is less than 0.05.

Generalised Linear Models

A Generalised Linear Model (GLM) is a generalisation of the linear bivariate regression model case. In its most simple form, it specifies the linear relationship between dependent (usually response) variables and a set of independent (predictor) variables. The GLM approach can be used to:

- Describe non-linear relationships between the dependent and independent variables,
- Describe the relationship between non-continuous dependent variables and independent variables.

The GLM is a simple modification to the linear regression case. A simplistic view of GLM is that it modifies a linear model by the addition of a link function. The type of link function chosen is based upon the assumed relationship between the dependent and independent variables. Link functions include normal, gamma, inverse normal and Poisson distributions.

In common with bivariate linear regression, the GLM technique shares difficulties in modelling data sets that contain strongly correlated predictor data. Further information regarding GLM is given in Statsoft. Relationships between categorical dependent and continuous data can be established using techniques such as logistic regression, logit and probit analysis. Further information regarding these techniques is given in Clogg and Stockley.

Artificial Neural Networks

In addition to classification of data, ANNs can be built to find relationships between X and Y data sets. These relationships may be linear or non-linear. The major disadvantage of the use of ANNs is that they do not provide the researcher with information regarding the statistical relationship between X and Y data sets.

Selection of Classification and Correlational Techniques

Decision-making was aided by performing a Kepner Tregoe decision analysis. This technique has four steps, outlined below.

Step 1: Identify those attributes of a desired option that are essential *musts* and those that are desirable *wants*. Enter the *musts* and *wants* into a matrix.

Step 2: Assess all of the options against all of the *musts*. Immediately reject any of the options that fail to meet all of the *musts*.

Step 3: Assess all of the options against their ability to meet the *wants*. Subjectively score the ability of the options to meet the each of the *wants*. If required, weight the relative importance of the attribute by multiplying the *want* score by a scalar.

Step 4: Totalise the *want* scores. The option with the highest *want* score is the preferred option.

In addition to aiding the decision-making process, the recording of the Kepner Tregoe matrix provides transparency to the subjective decision making process. The following paragraphs describe the decision analysis performed in order to select the most appropriate classification and correlational statistical techniques for detailed analysis.

Selection of Classification Techniques

Research questions 14 to 17 inclusive, listed in Table below require a classification technique to group objects (AstraZeneca sites) into categories based upon *a priori* knowledge of the object's performance, for example, injury frequency rates or the nation that a site belongs to. The chosen classification methodology must therefore be able to:

- Group objects based upon *a priori* classification knowledge.
- Deal with continuous predictor variables.
- Provide information regarding how strongly predictor variables influence an object's categorisation.

The desirable or *want* attributes of a classification technique are:

- Ease of model interpretation, preferably graphical in nature.
- The availability of support and expertise within AstraZeneca.
- The availability of software packages within AstraZeneca.

The above *musts* and *wants* are detailed in Table. The ability of the methodology to satisfy the *musts* was assessed and recorded in columns 2, 3 and 4. The ability of the methodologies to satisfy the *wants* was subjectively assessed by the author, and a score from 1 to 5 assigned, higher scores indicating desirable attributes. Methodologies not meeting all of the *must* attributes are not scored. The final column of Table provides a total score for the *wants*.

Table – Summary of classification statistical techniques

	Model *Musts*			Model *Wants*			
Method	**Can Classify Based Upon *a priori* Knowledge**	**Continuous Predictor Variables**	**Variable Importance Information Provided**	**Ease Of Model Interpretation**	**Software Available To Author**	**Support Available In AstraZeneca**	**Total**
PCA	"	!	!	-	-	-	-
PLS-DA	!	!	!	4	5	5	14
SIMCA	!	!	!	5	5	5	15
CA	!	!	!	2	3	5	10
SVM	!	!	!	2	3	5	10
KNN	!	!	!	2	3	5	10
CT	!	!	"	-	-	-	-
ANN	!	!	"	-	-	-	-
MDS	!	!	!	2	3	5	10

Inspection of Table indicates that the PCA, CT and ANN methodologies are unable to satisfy all of the *must* attributes of a classification methodology. The use of PCA, CT and ANN techniques was therefore rejected.

PLS-DA and SIMCA score more highly than the remaining classification methodologies due to the ease of model interpretation and the ready availability of the software to the author. SIMCA was scored marginally better than PLS-DA due to ease of model interpretation. The lower score of PLS-DA was assigned due to PLS-DA score and weightings plots being difficult to interpret when the number of classes exceeds five.

- It allowed inter-comparison of the effectiveness of the two methodologies.

- A software program capable of performing PLS-DA and SIMCA was available to the author.
- PLS-DA copes less well when there are five or more *a priori* classes. There may be a future requirement to discriminate between five or more classes.

Selection of Correlational Techniques

In addition to the *musts*, desirable or *want* attributes of the correlation technique include: Ease of model interpretation, preferably graphical in nature, The availability of support and expertise in AstraZeneca, The availability of software packages in AstraZeneca. Inspection of the model *wants* in Table 2.12 shows that PLS scores higher than MR and GLM. PLS is therefore the preferred and chosen method. The ultimate selection of PLS over MR and GLM was also significantly influenced by advice received from the AstraZeneca Statistical Science Group.

Selection of a statistical software package

With the exception of Artificial Neural Networks, it is possible to perform all of the techniques by manual calculation. However, the manual application of the techniques to the Focus 2002 data is not a practicable option due to the very large size of the data sets involved.

The use of a computer to perform the calculations is therefore essential. The literature review has shown that there are a great number of computer software programs available that are capable of performing the necessary calculations. Although the advent of computers and statistical programs has released researchers from the drudgery of calculations, their use gives rise to additional problems that can be overlooked. After learning the basics of using the program, including any associated programming language, the next most significant issue for the researcher is to understand the default program options and how and what the program does when it is run. According to Simpson there has been a recent upsurge in published material from researchers that have used statistical programs using default program options without justifying the reasons behind their selection. The ease of understanding the statistical program defaults and options is dependent upon the quality of supporting 'help' material that, in terms of quality and quantity, varies considerably from program to program. Another confounding problem for the researcher is the complexity of the statistical programs such as SAS-PRO CALIS (SAS Institute), LISREL, AMOS, SEPATH (Statistica) and EQS. Learning how to use these programs may take several months of practice. The availability of a suitable software programs can often significantly affect the researcher's selection of statistical technique. SIMCA P+ was selected as the statistical software program to perform the PLS, PLS-DA and SIMCA analysis to analyse the AstraZeneca Focus 2002 data. No other software programs were reviewed. SIMCA P+ was selected for the following reasons:

- The single program is capable of satisfying the two principal objectives of the research, namely, correlating Focus 2002 question responses with lagging SHE performance indicators and understanding the factors which discriminate the good and poor accident performing sites.
- It is capable of performing PCA, PLS, PLS-DA and SIMCA analysis.
- The graphical outputs from SIMCA P+ are easy to interpret.
- It is a preferred and extensively used statistical program within AstraZeneca.
- The ready availability of expert technical support and SIMCA P+ users.

SUMMARY AND CONCLUSIONS

SUMMARY OF CULTURE AND CLIMATE LITERATURE REVIEW

Research papers in the field of organisational safety culture and climate are plentiful. Organisational safety culture is seen as a subset of an organisation's overall culture. Like many social science constructs, organisational safety culture is multi-dimensional.

Since it is a construct, rather than a physical phenomenon, researchers can put forward their own theories of what culture is and how it operates. Because culture is multi-dimensional, several dimensions need to be simultaneously measured to accurately describe it. An organisation's safety culture is not directly perceivable by observers. However, its effects, such as the workers' attitudes, perceptions and behaviours are perceivable. The observable surface indicators of organisational culture are described as an organisation's climate. The most common way in which organisational safety climate is measured is via the administration of a safety climate survey.

Typically, these surveys consist of a number of questions, usually administered via a paper questionnaire, that probe the respondents' attitudes, perceptions and satisfactions regarding various organisational factors. Researchers often group the responses to the safety climate survey questions, based upon common associations in the way in which they were answered.

The process of identification of these common associations or factors is often accomplished by factor analysis statistical techniques. Researchers have proposed and labelled a significant number of organisational climate factors. However, a commonly agreed set of organisational safety climate factors does not exist, nor are they likely to within the foreseeable future. Existing research indicates that the number of climate factors that are claimed to be required to adequately describe an organisation's culture varies considerably. Different levels of culture exist and include group, organisational and national levels.

The relative inter-relationship and dominance of national, organisational and individual culture is unknown. The ability to use a single question-set to measure organisational culture across more than one nation may be significantly hindered by the dominance of national over organisational culture.

One or more groups of individuals within an organisation or nation may possess measurably different cultures. These different cultural groups are called sub-cultures. The likelihood of sub-cultures existing increases as the size of the organisation and the diversity of its operations increases. Some researchers have used the results of safety climate surveys to build a model of the factor associations and strength of inter-relationships between the factors. Structural equation modelling is often used to validate these models.

SUMMARY OF SHE PERFORMANCE METRICS

The apparent lack of available research that attempts to correlate metrics of organisational climate with SHE performance indicators is unsurprising. The lack of research in this area is probably due to the lack of available suitable metrics of SHE performance.

There are many SHE performance indicators used throughout the world. Several of these indicators are used in more than one country. An example of a commonly reported indicator is the 'accident frequency rate'. Although the indicator is common, the method of its calculation can vary between departments, functions, companies and nations. The existence of common reporting criteria is sometimes insufficient to ensure consistent reporting. An example of this problem is in the classification of injuries that go into injury frequency rate calculations. Within the SHE profession, definition of what constitutes a minor injury may vary considerably.

In one company a paper cut may be classified as a minor injury, whereas in another company such an incident may be an unclassified event or even disregarded altogether. In the absence of precise guidance on the classification of, in this instance, injuries, the number of degrees of interpretive freedom will give rise to inconsistent reporting.

The consistency of injury reports is inversely related to the number of interpretive degrees of freedom. The principles of the loss prevention triangle where the ratio between successive injury type decreases rapidly from near-miss to minor, to major, through to deaths is well established and accepted by safety professionals around the world.

It is suggested that the degree of interpretive freedom decreases, and therefore the cross-correlational robustness increases, as the severity of incidents increases. This suggestion may explain why injuries at the minor end of the reporting spectrum are often perceived to be under-reported. Those incidents that are less likely to be under-reported are accidents resulting in death and serious injury, fires and explosions, occupational illnesses, external complaints by members of the public, non-compliance with SHE licences, permits and consents, and legal sanctions.

These incidents are likely to be accurately reported, as the degree of freedom to interpret the reporting criteria is low. Incidents such as accidents leading to damage to property resulting in business interruption, accidents leading to damage to the environment and accidents that could have, but did not result in, a serious injury or death, damage to property leading to business interruption, and damage to the environment, are all likely to be incorrectly reported due to higher degrees of interpretative freedom. Decreasing the number of degrees of interpretative freedom of a reporting requirement may not be sufficient to ensure adequate comparisons. The presence of procedures and prescriptive guidance does not necessarily guarantee that all incidents are correctly reported.

Other factors such as the organisational culture, sub-cultures and the way in which adherence to procedures is monitored and enforced may significantly affect the reliability of the data produced. National, organisational and functional group culture may have a significant impact on the robustness of SHE performance indicators.

A trivial example of functional group culture would be a scaffolder and an office worker both of whom suffered a paper cut. Due to the 'macho' culture of the construction industry, it is highly unlikely that a scaffolder, even in the presence of procedures and guidance, would bring the incident to the attention of the business. Due to the number of degrees of interpretative freedom outlined above, adherence to an incident reporting procedure will increase as the severity of the incident increases.

It is highly unlikely that a significant accident such as a death or a broken leg would go unreported. In conclusion, researchers attempting to compare groups or organisations based upon SHE performance indicators must have a thorough understanding of the criteria and guidance used to produce them, be mindful of the number of degrees of interpretive freedom and have regard to differences in national and organisational culture that may give rise to biased reporting.

This procedure appears, so far as is reasonably practicable, to address the issues highlighted above, in that reporting criteria are well defined in writing and are supported by management procedures. Due to the reasons outlined above it would appear that correlations of serious incidents with organisational climate factors would provide a more robust metric than that between minor accident rates and organisational climate factors. This assumption would hold true only if the number of serious incidents on a site are frequent enough to give rise to statistically significant correlations.

The Bird and Germain loss prevention triangle informs us that the ratio between 'serious or major injury' to 'minor injuries' to 'property damage accidents' to 'incidents with no visible injury or damage' is 1:10:30:600. The frequency of occurrence of the high consequence incidents may therefore be too low to allow statistically significant analysis. If De Cock et al's assumption that organisational culture is stable over a period of five years or so is correct, then there may be potential benefit in adding the accident statistics of two or more years to obtain a more statistically robust data set. The reported indicators should reflect reality. Formally reported and recorded indicators should be used in preference to informal or 'recollected' data. The use of self-reported accidents and injury data is questionable for a number of reasons including the following:

The definitions and thresholds of self-reported accidents and injuries are often ambiguous and open to respondent's interpretation.

Due to lack of a formal record keeping and individual respondent's recollection, the number and seriousness of incidents reported may be inaccurate.

A person's threshold of accident self-reporting may be influenced by the organisational climate. It is reasonable to assume that an individual's self-reporting threshold would be proportional to his perception and attitudes towards the organisational climate. Investigating the correlation of self-reported accident/injury data with actual accident records, how these may vary with time and be influenced by organisational factors, would be a topical area that would benefit from future research.

The literature search associated with climate issues was almost entirely related to safety events such as self-reported injury rates, RIDDOR events and various metrics of risk. No research literature was found that attempted to correlate organisational climate factors with environmental performance indicators such as number of uncontrolled environmental releases. As environmental incidents may readily occur without being noticed, the accurate measurement of lagging environmental performance indicators are potentially more troublesome than lagging safety performance indicators.

The comparison of environmental performance indicators across departments, functions, sites, industries and nations is hampered by the lack of common terms of reference and definitions. At first sight, the likelihood of common reporting criteria being created may seem low. The enabling framework to move towards common reporting criteria is, however, arguably already present in the form of the International Standards Organisation (ISO).

ISO prescribes a number of accredited standards on various subject areas, one of which includes ISO 14001. The adoption by industry of a common reporting terminology, such as that prescribed in recognised standards, would facilitate convergence and hence improve the current situation.

The ability of an organisational culture survey tool to identify sub-populations with anomalous traits diminishes as the population increases. A non-uniform population may have a desired mean organisational culture indicator. However, its SHE performance, using lagging indicators, may be dominated by a minority with non-desired culture indicators. The use of mean culture indicators is of use only when it is known that the mean reflects the majority of the population. All of the research reviewed that attempted to correlate culture indicators with SHE performance used mean values of culture indicators, without having regard to the distribution around the mean.

Summary of Correlating Organisational Climate Metrics to Safety Performance

Much research is available that has found statistically significant correlation between *single* aspects of organisational climate with SHE lagging indicators and other outcomes.

A significant amount of research has examined the multi-dimensional structure of organisational climate and how it can be measured. No research was found in the literature review that has successfully correlated several dimensions of organisational culture, at the same time, with SHE or other business outcomes.

The work done by Zohar was the only research identified that has attempted to correlate several dimensions of organisational climate, at the same time, with a SHE outcome. Although Zohar claimed to have produced a model that is able to provide significant prediction of accident rate, his model was only able to account for 16% of the observed accident data variation. Due to its poor predictive ability, Zohar's model would be rejected by industry.

Four fundamental issues need to be addressed to enable a link between organisational culture constructs and lagging SHE performance indicators to be made, namely:

- A set of metrics are required to be identified that adequately describe the organisational culture at all of the sites to be compared.

- All groups being compared with one another must have comparable SHE performance indicators.
- The chosen SHE performance indicators must be able to discriminate the groups being compared.
- There must be a sufficient number of groups to allow statistically significant relationships to be drawn.

The Applicability of Existing Research to AstraZeneca

The literature review has confirmed that existing research has not:

Successfully established a simultaneous link between several dimensions of organisational culture and SHE lagging performance indicators.

Used a multi-dimensional organisational culture model to identify those organisational attributes correlated to SHE outcomes.

Applied PLS to correlate the multi-dimensional nature of organisational culture with organisational outcomes.

Applied SIMCA or PLS-DA methodologies to identify those organisational culture attributes that correlate with organisational outcomes.

Application of PLS, PLS-DA and SIMCA methodologies to the Focus 2002 survey responses and GSHE 2002 data will aim to answer research questions 8 to 17 inclusive listed in Table.

Answering these questions will significantly advance current knowledge and understanding in the field of organisational culture and its relationship to SHE outcomes.

RECOMMENDATIONS FOR FURTHER WORK

Throughout this research project, questions have arisen which lie outside its scope, but which, if answered, would significantly advance the understanding, knowledge, and practical application of organisational culture metrics within industry. The recommendations for further work are as follows:

- Investigate the stability of organisational culture with time.
- Investigate whether the correlation between organisational culture and significant-injury frequency rates is stable over a period of several years.
- Perform research to find out the extent to which accident rates drive organisational culture and visa versa.
- Examine the relationship between organisational climate metrics and other business outputs such as productivity and quality metrics.
- Further develop the vision of a single tool that takes several different types of organisational measurements into consideration in order to predict SHE performance.
- Investigate the integration of organisational culture metrics into a relative risk ranking methodology, which takes into account several facets associated with SHE performance.
- Perform PLS, PL-DA and SIMCA analysis on subsequent AstraZeneca Focus surveys in order to find a common set of question responses that correlate with safety in the United Kingdom, Sweden and the United States.
- Explore the usefulness of artificial neural networks in revealing the relationships between organisational climate metrics and lagging SHE performance indicators.

- Explore whether national culture dominates over organisational culture in multi-national climate surveys.
- Promote the usefulness of the measurement of organisational culture throughout AstraZeneca.
- Collect organisational culture data from personnel who have experienced an accident and those who have not. Perform discriminant analysis on the information in order to identify the factors that are associated with those who have accidents.
- Investigate the relationship between the degree of risk a person is subjected to and the likelihood of that person being involved in an undesired SHE outcome.
- Investigate the relationship between organisational sub-cultures and the likelihood of an individual belonging to the sub-culture having an accident.
- Incorporate the 'behavioural' and 'safety management system' elements of Cooper's model of safety culture into a PLS model.

BIBLIOGRAPHY

Alfred, H.: *Hospitality Design for the Graying Generation: Meeting the Needs of a Growing Market,* New York, Wiley, 1996.

Allcock, R.S.: *Development Training: A Personal View,* Birmingham, Endeavour Training, 1988.

Asch, D.: *Managing Strategy,* Basingstoke, MacMillan Press Ltd, 1996.

Bandura, A.: *Social Learning and Personality Development,* New York, Holt, Rinehart, and Winston, 1963.

Bronstein, P. A.: *Teaching a Psychology of People,* Washington, American Psychological Association, 1988.

Damon, William: *Social and Personality Development: Infancy through Adolescence,* New York, Norton, 1983.

Denhardt, R. B.: *Managing Human Behavior in Public & Nonprofit Organizations,* Thousand Oaks, Sage, 2002.

Eberts, Marjorie: *Careers in Travel, Tourism, and Hospitality,* Lincolnwood, VGM Career Horizons, 1997.

Gilligan, C. with Pearson, D. J.: *Strategic Marketing Management,* Oxford, Butterworth-Heinemann Ltd., 1992.

Greenaway, R.: *The Training and Development of Development Trainers,* Ambleside, Brathay Hall Trust, 1986.

Hoffman, Edward: *Project Management Success Stories: Lessons of Project Leaders,* New York, John Wiley & Son, 2000.

Ireland, Lewis: *Quality Management for Projects and Programs,* Upper Darby, PMI, 1991.

Jarvis, R.: *Business Accounting for Hospitality and Tourism*, London, Chapman and Hall, 1995.

John, B.: *Temperament: Individual Differences at the Interface of Biology and Behavior,* Washington, American Psychological Association, 1994.

Johnson, Hazel: *Financial Institutions and Markets: A Global Perspective,* NY, McGraw Hill, 1993.

Kenneth, R.: *Social, Emotional, and Personality Development,* New York, Wiley, 1998.

Koontz, H.: *Management: A Global Perspective*, New York, McGraw Hill, 1993.

Lawrence J.: *Principles of Managerial Finance*, MA: Addison Wesley Longman, 2000.

Lock, Dennis: *Project Management,* New York, Wiley, 1996.

Martin: *Basic Financial Management*, Prentice Hall, 1993.

Pender, Lesley: *Marketing Management for Travel and Tourism*, Cheltenham, Stanley Thornes Publishers, 1999.

Rosemary, E.: *Managing Employee Relations in the Hotel and Catering Industry*, London, Cassell, 1995.

Stallworthy, E.: *Waste Management Towards a Sustainable Society*, Auburn House, New York, 1990.

Stephens, G. L.: *Philosophical Psychopathology*, Cambridge, MIT Press, 1994.

William, D.: *Social and Personality Development: Infancy through Adolescence,* New York, Norton, 1983.

Index

♦♦♦